Coaching

Also by Lin Carver

Reading Basics for All Teachers: Supporting the Common Core

Coaching

Making a Difference for K–12 Students and Teachers

Lin Carver and Judith Orth

Rowman & Littlefield
Lanham • Boulder • New York • London

Published by Rowman & Littlefield
A wholly owned subsidiary of The Rowman & Littlefield Publishing Group, Inc.
4501 Forbes Boulevard, Suite 200, Lanham, Maryland 20706
www.rowman.com

Unit A, Whitacre Mews, 26-34 Stannary Street, London SE11 4AB

Copyright © 2017 by Lin Carver and Judith Orth

All rights reserved. No part of this book may be reproduced in any form or by any electronic or mechanical means, including information storage and retrieval systems, without written permission from the publisher, except by a reviewer who may quote passages in a review.

British Library Cataloguing in Publication Information Available

Library of Congress Cataloging-in-Publication Data Available

ISBN 9781475833003 (cloth : alk. paper)
ISBN 9781475833034 (pbk. : alk. paper)
ISBN 9781475833041 (electronic)

∞™ The paper used in this publication meets the minimum requirements of American National Standard for Information Sciences—Permanence of Paper for Printed Library Materials, ANSI/NISO Z39.48-1992.

Printed in the United States of America

CONTENTS

CHAPTER ONE 1
What Is Coaching? 2
    Six Definitions of Coaching 3
    Coaching Is Voluntary 4
    Approaches to Coaching 5
What Is a Growth Mindset? 5
    Developing a Growth Mindset 6
    Hindrances to a Growth Mindset 7
    Staying Positive around Negative People 8
    Working Together 9
SMART Goals 10
    Specific Goal 10
    Measurable Goal 10
    Attainable Goal 11
    Realistic Goal 11
    Timely Goal 11
Reflect and Apply Activities 12
References 12

CHAPTER TWO 15
Teacher Effectiveness 16
    Characteristics of Effective Teachers as Determined by
        Teachers' Perception 16
    Characteristics of Effective Teachers as Determined by
        Student Achievement 17

CONTENTS

Effective Coaches 18
    PBWorks's Characteristics of Effective Coaches 18
Coaching and Supervision 20
    Coaching Is Not Supervision 20
Components of Coaching 21
    Relationship Skills 22
    Leadership Skills 22
    Content Area Skills 22
    Literacy Skills 22
    Assessment Skills 23
    Writing Skills 23
    Differentiation Skills 23
    Adult Learning Skills 24
Reflect and Apply Activities 25
References 25

CHAPTER THREE 27
Categories of Teachers 28
Processing Information 29
Short-Term Memory 29
    Working Memory 30
    Increasing Working Memory 31
Long-Term Memory 31
Moving Information from Short-Term to Long-Term Memory 32
    Self-Concept 33
    Humor 33
Teaching Implications 33
Reflect and Apply Activities 34
References 34

CHAPTER FOUR 37
Leadership Characteristics 38
    Comparing Characteristics of Effective Coaches 38
Data Analysis 39
Disaggregation 40
    Trend 40
    Cohort 41
    Longitudinal 42
Data Provides the Basis for the Coaching Process 42
Professional Development 43
    Adult Learners 43

CONTENTS

Learning Improves Our Brain 43
Long-Term Memory 44
Types of Long-Term Memory 44
    Declarative Memory 45
    Nondeclarative Memory 45
Application 46
Reflect and Apply Activities 46
References 47

CHAPTER FIVE 49
Learning Climate 50
Retention 51
    Rote Rehearsal 51
    Elaborative Rehearsal 51
    Serial Position Effect 52
    Instructional Methods 52
    Multisensory Approaches 52
Learning and Motor Skills 53
Factors Impacting Retrieval Rates 53
Structuring Professional Development 54
Using the Gradual Release Model to Plan Professional Development 55
    Establish the Purpose 55
    I Do 55
    We Do 56
    We Do Together 56
    You Do 57
    Reflection 57
Types of Coaching 57
    Informal Coaching Model 57
    Mixed Model of Informal and Formal Coaching 58
    Formal Literacy Coaching Model 58
    Peer Coaching and Mentoring Model 58
    Cognitive Coaching Model 58
    Clinical Supervision Model 59
Coaching Continuum of Learning Formats 59
Reflect and Apply Activities 61
References 61

CHAPTER SIX 63
Methods of Data Collection 65
Formal and Informal Assessments 65

CONTENTS

- Norm- and Criterion-Referenced Assessments 66
- Types of Formal Assessments 66
  - Screening Assessments 67
  - Diagnostic Assessments 67
  - Progress-Monitoring Assessments 68
  - Summative/Evaluative/Outcome Assessments 68
- Types of Informal Assessments 68
- Levels of Data Analysis 69
  - School and District Data 69
  - Class Data 69
  - Student Data 69
- Can Instruction Really Make a Difference? 70
- Collecting Teacher Data 71
  - Anonymous or Identified 72
  - Response Type 72
  - Structuring Questions 72
  - Question Order 73
- Reflect and Apply Activities 73
- References 74

CHAPTER SEVEN 77
- Learning Styles of Children and Adults 78
  - Visual Learners 79
  - Kinesthetic Learners 79
  - Auditory Learners 80
- Gardner's Intelligences 80
- Adult Learning Theories 82
  - Andragogy 82
  - Self-Directed Learning 82
  - Transformative Learning 83
- Professional Development 83
- Coaching Practices 84
- Observational Categories 84
- Using Data from Observations 85
- Teacher Evaluation Systems 86
- Reflect and Apply Activities 88
- References 90

CHAPTER EIGHT 93
- Components of a Well-Designed Coaching System 94
  - Content-Based Focus on Adult Learning 95

CONTENTS

    Conditions That Support Effective Coaching 96
    Instructional Leadership Provided by the Coach 97
Teachers at Different Career Stages. 97
Working with Teachers 98
Feedback. 99
    Specific Praise. 99
    Instructional Scaffolding 99
    Corrective Feedback 100
Reflect and Apply Activities 101
References 101

CHAPTER NINE 103
Teaching Digital Natives. 104
    Task Switching 105
    Complex Texts. 105
    Use of Novelty. 106
    Use of Humor 106
    Use of Movement. 106
Lesson Preparation. 107
    Incorporate Digital Resources. 107
    Don't Overload Information 107
    Lesson Preparation and Teacher Evaluation Systems. 108
Professional Learning Communities. 109
Keys to Effective Coaching 109
Listening Skills. 110
    Level 1: Internal Listening 110
    Level 2: Focused Listening 111
    Level 3: Global Listening 111
Use of Silence. 112
Minimal Encouragers 112
    Verbal Listening Skills. 112
Questioning 113
    Using Questions in the Coaching Session. 113
Reflect and Apply Activities 114
References 115

CHAPTER TEN 117
Classroom Environment. 118
Physical Environment 119
    Lighting 119
    Noise. 120

CONTENTS

  Temperature. 120
  Room Arrangement 120
  Traffic Flow. 121
  Visual Displays 121
 Social/Cultural Environment 121
  Teacher–Student Interactions 122
  Peer Interactions 122
  Respect Is Evident 122
  Student Expectations Clearly Stated 123
  Multicultural Materials Used 123
  Classroom Management. 123
 Instructional Environment 124
  Organization 124
  Student Involvement. 124
  Differentiation 124
  Transitions 125
  Student Achievement Is Valued. 125
 Providing Feedback after an Observation 125
  Grade-Level Concerns. 126
  Setting the Teacher at Ease. 126
  Teacher Respect. 126
  Structuring Feedback 126
 Reflect and Apply Activities. 127
 References 128

CHAPTER ELEVEN. 131
 Bloom's Taxonomy 133
  Levels of Higher-Order Thinking. 133
  Encouraging Higher-Order Thinking. 134
  Thinking and Emotion 134
  Difference between Complexity and Difficulty. 135
 Working with Resistant Teachers 135
  Avoiding a Top-Down Process 135
  Peer Coaching 136
  Action Research. 136
  Make Them Part of a Group. 136
 Steps in the Action Research Process. 137
 Providing Support. 137
 Reflect and Apply Activities. 138
 References 139

CONTENTS

CHAPTER TWELVE 141
   Classroom Management. 142
   Establishing Classroom Rules. 142
      Specific Rules 143
      General Rules. 143
   Procedures and Routines. 143
   Individual Intervention Strategies. 144
      Point Sheets 144
      Observing a Student. 145
      ABC Chart 145
      Off-Task Behavior Chart 145
   Reflect and Apply Activities 147
   References 148

CHAPTER THIRTEEN 149
   Tips for Beginning Coaches 150
   Developing Skills. 152
   Coaching Support. 153
   Professional Development to Change Practice. 153
   Reflect and Apply Activities. 154
   References 154

APPENDIXES
   Appendix A: Evaluating Instruction Short-Term Memory Checklist 157
   Appendix B: Evaluating Instruction Short- and Long-Term Memory Checklist. ... 159
   Appendix C: Checklist for Moran's Continuum of Learning Formats 161
   Appendix D: Basic Literacy Data-Collection Tool 163
   Appendix E: Literacy Data Collection by Standard. 165
   Appendix F: K–5 Mathematics Data-Collection Tool. 167
   Appendix G: 6–8 Mathematics Data-Collection Tool 169
   Appendix H: Environmental Observation Form 171
   Appendix I: Higher-Order Question Stems and Projects 173
   Appendix J: Weekly Point Sheet 177
   Appendix K: ABC Chart 179
   Appendix L: Off-Task Behavior Chart. 181

Index. 183
About the Author 187

CHAPTER ONE

It was the beginning of a new school year, and as the faculty meandered into the media center on their first day of preplanning week, they greeted old friends and shared exploits from their summer vacations. Jessie sat in the back of the room. This was her first day as a faculty member on this campus, and she did not know anyone. Three weeks earlier she had responded to an advertisement for an academic coach. After spending the last eight years teaching fifth grade, she thought she was ready for a change. The interview with the principal had been interesting. They had talked about all that he hoped to accomplish during this school year, the challenges the school had faced last year, and his excitement about being able to get funds to pay for the new position of academic coach. He had never had an academic coach before, but he had read about them and had managed to convince the district that because of the concerns at his school they needed one.

Now, sitting in the back of the media center listening, Jessie could hear all the teachers talking excitedly about setting up their rooms. She had not considered the challenge of coaching teachers with whom she did not have a relationship. She began to second-guess her decision to take the coaching job at Smith Elementary.

Smith Elementary was a school with 84 percent of students receiving free and reduced lunch and a large ELL population of Hispanic students. She thought back to her previous school, with its 21 percent free and reduced-lunch population and only a handful of Spanish-speaking students. She thought about the fourth graders she had known last year and

CHAPTER ONE

how she had been looking forward to teaching them. She had known most of them since kindergarten and had watched them grow up. She sighed, realizing she would really miss them.

Her thoughts shifted to this new job she had taken. She wondered exactly what her academic coaching position would entail. Would the faculty be receptive toward her? Would she know how to help these students and teachers be successful? The more she thought about it, the more she was filled with self-doubt. Did she know enough to be successful in this position? Her mind wandered as the rest of the faculty stopped milling around and settled nosily into their seats. Finally, the noise dwindled as the principal stepped up to the podium.

"Welcome back to the home of the Bears. It is great to see you all. We are going to have a wonderful year!" the principal greeted them enthusiastically. *I hope so*, Jessie thought. What would she be doing this year in her new coaching role?

What Is Coaching?

Coaching occurs daily in both formal and informal relationships in many different settings. Experienced teachers are involved in coaching, whether it is helping the beginning teacher next door, working with colleagues, or actually filling the role of the academic coach like Jessie is. But coaching does not occur only with other teachers. A teacher coaches a student by encouraging him to do his best work. A parent works with her child to help her overcome some hurdles in her life. We realize that all of these are coaching situations. But what exactly is coaching? How do you coach and what do you need to know to be able to do it effectively? These are important questions to consider.

Coaching occurs in sports, businesses, schools, and in many other arenas. The idea of coaching has been around since the 1800s. The word "coach" was derived from "Kosc," which was the name of a Hungarian village that was famous for producing quality coaches. "Coach" was originally used as a slang term by students to describe the English university tutors who were so efficient that it seemed like they "carried" their students through their exams (Wilson, 2004). The university students' slang use of the word "coaching" lead to the idea of a coach being able to take a person from where they were to where they wanted to be. The term "coach" has been used in education for hundreds of years. However, coaching has certainly not been limited to education. Coaches abound in all areas: career coaching, life coaching, business coaching, financial coaching, homework coaching, relationship coaching, health coaching, and, of course, sports coaching, just to name a few.

According to *Webster's Ninth New Collegiate Dictionary* (Merriam-Webster, 1986), coaching is defined as "to train intensively" as by instruction and demonstration (p. 253). "Instructional coaching" in education is providing focused support to classroom teachers, helping them achieve the goals that they have set for students through the implementation of research-based practices. Coaching can also help educators and administrators contextualize goals or district practices through professional development workshops or seminars, with the ultimate goal of having the teachers apply the newly gained knowledge in their own classrooms.

A "coach" in an educational setting can use the inquiry approach to determine strengths, goals, and questions related to student learning that teachers have in relation to their own classroom. Using their personal expertise, the coach will determine how to appropriately answer the teachers' questions and decide what type of guidance, information, or scaffolding would be needed to help the teachers achieve their classroom goals. Coaches may address specific issues of content area curriculum, content instruction and standards (including incorporating Common Core Standards into the district curriculum), or instructional practices. Whatever educational issues or concerns the teacher is experiencing, the coach needs to be able to address the specific needs of the teacher.

Six Definitions of Coaching

The coaching process is complex and encompasses many different components and perspectives. Often, the coach is viewed as the expert who can provide direction to an individual wishing to learn more. In this type of an approach, the coach takes the actions needed to help the other person achieve the desired changes (Stephens & Mills, 2014). Feiman-Nemser (1996), however, focused on support for beginning teachers and used the terms "coach" and "mentor" interchangeably. A mentor or coach was described as an experienced teacher who worked with novice teachers using more extensive knowledge to help the novice teachers improve their practice. In this view, the mentor would then be the source of support for beginning teachers.

Lyons and Pinnell (2001) expanded on this perspective of coaching by including all teachers rather than focusing on just beginning teachers. They defined coaches as individuals who could see past what was currently happening in the classroom. The coach needed to be able to identify how to improve instructional practices by helping all teachers expand their knowledge base, while providing support and encouragement.

Spaulding and Smith (2012) further expanded the role of instructional coach to include staff and administration rather than just focusing on teachers. They described a coach as an individual who "works directly and indirectly with teachers, staff, and building principals to improve the effectiveness of classroom instruction and increase student learning, performance, and overall achievement" (p. 1). They placed the coach in the role of an expert. However, in an alternate view, Puig and Froelich (2007) moved the coach out of the expert role and into that of a co-learner with teachers. They describe the coach's role as a support teacher who facilitated growth, since both the coach and the teacher continued to develop in their educational practice.

Hasbrouck and Denton (2005) provided a different perspective on the role of the coach. They shifted the focus of the coaching role from the teacher to the student. Hasbrouck and Denton developed a student-focused coaching model that takes the emphasis off of the teacher and moves the focus squarely on student achievement. They developed a student-focused coaching model that they defined as a "cooperative, ideally collaborative relationship, with parties mutually engaged in efforts to provide better services for students" (p. 2). "Coaching," though a frequently used term, has been explained and implemented in many different ways.

Coaching Is Voluntary

No matter which approach to coaching is endorsed in your setting, the coaching process needs to be based on a voluntary relationship. The coach cannot coach someone who does not want to be coached. After considering all of these descriptions of the coaching process, we propose that the emphasis of the coaching process should be on both teacher and student growth. These are intertwined and difficult to separate as one impacts the other. Effective teacher growth will result in student growth.

Approaches to Coaching

Even when the coaching efforts focus on student growth, the coach's activities occur in at least three different ways. Coaches might be facilitators who help skilled teachers continue in their commitment to help all students be successful. In this role the coach is providing direct instruction for the teacher. When acting as the facilitator, the coach is more in the expert role than in the co-learner role. The coach might also act as a collaborative problem solver who uses a systematic, structured process to help teachers address the problems or challenges that are keeping students from being successful. Finally, the coach could be a teacher/learner working alongside of the teacher to share effective practices through both individual and group professional development. In the typical school setting, depending on teachers' needs, the different approaches to coaching are not separated and the coaching role encompasses all three of these facets.

What Is a Growth Mindset?

No matter which approach to coaching a school chooses, the coaching process needs to be based on a growth mindset. It would be pointless for an athlete to work with a coach if the athlete and the coach did not both think the athlete could improve by implementing the coach's suggestions. For coaching to be most effective, teachers, students, and the coach all need a growth rather than a fixed mindset. But what exactly is a growth mindset?

Dweck's (2006) work identified the difference between a growth and a fixed mindset. In a fixed mindset, people believe their basic qualities of intelligence and talent are fixed traits. In other words, individuals have a specific amount of intelligence and talent they were born with, and that is all they will ever have. These innate qualities of intelligence and talent are what determine whether individuals are successful. If individuals are not successful, it is because they did not have enough talent and ability. In other words, the lack of success is due to a mismatch between the individual's talents and the talents needed in that particular situation.

CHAPTER ONE

In a growth mindset, people believe that their intellect and talents are a starting point. They believe these abilities can be developed through dedication and hard work. The adoption of this growth mindset results in a love of learning and a resilience that enables learners to accomplish many new things that they were not capable of accomplishing before. They are not limited by their innate intelligence, talents, and abilities.

Do you have a growth or a fixed mindset? Consider the three following sentences and determine which one best describes your feelings.

1. A person cannot significantly change his level of talent or intelligence.
2. A person can learn new things, but he can't really change the amount of talent or intelligence he has.
3. A person can significantly change his level of intelligence and talent.

Each statement represents a different perspective or mindset. As you have probably figured out, statement number 3 reflects the growth mindset. If you are viewing individuals with a growth mindset, you are more likely to support and expect a change in their attitudes and abilities. If you don't have a growth mindset, this deficit may hinder you as a coach when you try to help others reach their full potential.

Developing a Growth Mindset

What attitudes should educators cultivate to encourage a growth mindset? These attitudes center around a "can do" perspective toward technology, relationships, resources, overcoming adversity, and taking risks. Heick (2013) identified nine statements for teaching and coaching to help to develop a growth mindset.

- I can use technology to make both my own and my students' learning richer.
- I can risk trying new learning activities.
- I can bring my own and my students' passions into learning activities.

- I can make one small change at a time in my learning environment.
- I can let go of my need to control all variables.
- I can find ways to change even under adversity.
- I value my relationships with my students (even over content).
- I can network and connect with others for resources, assistance, and support.
- I can make a difference in students' lives (para. 5).

In this age of standards-based education, teachers are constantly encouraged to change, grow, and differentiate in order to better meet the needs of their students. Educators are required to analyze school grades, achievement data, and information from progress-monitoring assessments. They are involved in many different professional development opportunities and are required to identify deliberate practices to enhance their instruction. These are all great activities. However, there has not been as much direction provided about how to determine what the most effective changes would be.

Consequently, teachers are faced with many questions they need to answer. How should teachers determine what kind of change will bring about the best results for their students? The data points to the problem, but teachers need to determine the most effective solution or change to attempt to implement. In other words, *exactly* how should the teacher go about making the change? What types of actions will bring about the desired change most effectively? Since coaching focuses on growth, it is important to develop a growth mindset. Coaches need to determine what types of internal or external coaching to use to establish the kind of thinking that promotes a growth mindset for teachers and their students.

Hindrances to a Growth Mindset

Two of the greatest hindrances to developing a growth mindset might be how comfortable the teacher is in the situation and the effects of negative teachers around them. To illustrate this concept, consider the following: When you are relaxing in your favorite chair at home, how anxious are you to change that situation? Probably not very anxious. If the teacher is comfortable in the situation, there is no desire or reason to change.

However, even if you want to change, negative people around you can also impact your desire to change. Negative people can be either an impetus for change or a deterrent to change. If you spend time around people who are always telling you that it is the parents' fault or the environment's fault that these students "can't learn," you can quickly fall into the habit of thinking that there is nothing you can do to change the situation. However, if you are tired of hearing that "these students can't learn," those words might encourage you to look for ways to correct the situation.

Staying Positive around Negative People

Being around negative people might impact you in different ways depending on whether you have a fixed or a growth mindset. Even though we would really not like to admit it, negative people are in every school or setting. Consequently, the coach will need strategies for dealing with them without becoming discouraged by them. How can the coaches stay positive while dealing with the few negative people that are at their school?

The first step, and maybe the most important one for staying positive when dealing with negative people, is to ensure a growth mindset. The coach needs to realize that everyone can change, so it is important to really listen to what the person is saying. Listen to the words, but don't stop there. Try to determine what the person really means. What factors are causing the individual to respond in a negative way? Often when others are talking, we are so busy forming our answer that we don't really hear what they are saying. This can lead to misunderstandings.

When you are tempted to get irritated with other's negative responses, a great step toward deterring these thoughts is to have some simple questions ready to ask. Some questions you might consider could be: "Can you tell me more? Why do you think that? Can you explain more specifically?" These questions will enable you to develop a better understanding of the person's perspective while encouraging him to think and respond more specifically in an attempt to support or clarify his position. This information might help you to pinpoint the exact difficulties that are occurring so that you can better support a change. But sometimes you just don't know how to respond to those negative people around you and the questions don't seem quite right. In that case, you might try something as simple as "Thank you for sharing; I need to think more about that." This type of response will give you time to collect more data about the situation without committing yourself (Vogt & Shearer, 2011).

Working Together

Using the growth mindset, the coach's goal is to improve academic achievement for all students through providing strong and consistent instructional leadership and support for the teachers. This is usually most effective when the academic coach works closely with the school's administration and the instructional leadership team. Together, more can be accomplished.

The instructional leadership team is typically composed of at least one of the school's administrators, the coach, and teacher and staff representatives. These parties can work together to establish the coach's job description, role, and responsibilities, as well as an action plan for the school. In order for the coach to be effective, it is important that both teachers and staff are aware of the coach's roles and responsibilities. But in our scenario, Jessie has not met the instructional leadership team. She has only met the principal, who has not yet fully defined her responsibilities. He is just excited to have an academic coach. The day-to-day realities of the coaching job have not been fleshed out.

During Jessie's interview, a lot of general ideas were talked about, but few specifics were discussed. As Jessie sat in the media center on the first day of school, she was concerned about what her responsibilities would be and what she would be doing each day. When she was preparing for the interview, she had read that the coach was NOT supposed to be a substitute teacher, administrator, paraprofessional, lunch supervisor, faculty evaluator, discipline dean, clerical assistance, resource teacher, special education teacher, or part of the administration. But the principal had not yet explained exactly what she was supposed to be doing or what she was supposed to be accomplishing.

CHAPTER ONE

SMART Goals

In her previous school, Jessie had learned about a growth mindset and had experienced it firsthand. As she started her role in this new school, she believed that these teachers and students could be very successful and that student achievement could improve. But how should she go about it; what should her first steps be?

Since Jessie has enthusiastically embraced teacher and student growth, this might be the time for her to start to develop some specific growth plans for herself, too. She cannot cause others to grow, but she can develop plans that include the steps she will follow to become an effective coach. To further develop her coaching abilities based on her growth mindset, now would be a great time to develop specific SMART goals (Top Achievement, n.d.) for her professional growth as a coach.

Although student growth is the ultimate goal, Jessie needs to establish SMART goals for her personal growth as a coach. Reaching her personal SMART goals will enable her to better serve both students and teachers by expanding her knowledge and skills. The SMART goals that she develops need to be *specific, measurable, attainable, realistic,* and *timely*.

Specific Goal

In order for the goal to be specific, it needs to answer the six *W*s: who, what, when, where, which, and why. Jessie knows that if someone reads her SMART goal, they should be able to determine the steps she is going to take to reach that goal. She has learned that "To lose weight" is not a specific goal. It is a great beginning, but the goal needs to be even more specific and focus on the steps she would follow to reach it. A better goal would be: "For the next two months, I will work out for fifteen minutes at the YMCA three times a week." That would be much more specific. Now she needs to take this understanding and apply it to her new school setting to develop a SMART goal that is specific to her role as a coach.

Measurable Goal

To determine whether the goal is measurable, Jessie would need to ask herself how she would know if the goal were accomplished. When she constructs her goal, it should have a specific frequency, length of time, or number of repetitions so that it can be measured. For example, if Jessie's goal is to work out at the YMCA for fifteen minutes three times a week for a month so that she can lose five pounds, her goal would be measurable. From her goal statement, it is easy to determine the length of time, the frequency, and the duration of the activity she identified.

Attainable Goal

Jessie needs to determine the personal importance of her SMART goal. Is her SMART goal something that she really could attain within the time frame? If it is too big, she might need to break the SMART goal down into smaller steps or goals. For example, if Jessie wishes to lose twenty pounds by going to the YMCA three times a week for two weeks, her goal might not be attainable. However, if we know that in the past she has gone to the YMCA for fifteen minutes three times a week for four weeks and lost five pounds, Jessie's attainable goal should be to work out at the YMCA fifteen minutes three times a week for sixteen weeks. If she follows this regime, Jessie should lose her desired twenty pounds; this is an attainable goal for her.

Realistic Goal

Jessie needs to determine whether her goal is realistic. Is the SMART goal she decides to develop one that she is willing and able to work to attain? She thought about that weight analogy again. Jessie might want to lose five pounds in a month or twenty pounds in four months. However, it will be attainable only if she is willing to make the effort to go to the YMCA three times a week for the four months. If Jessie is not willing to go to the YMCA three times a week for several months, she will not lose her desired weight, so it would not be realistic.

Timely Goal

Finally, Jessie thought, the goal must have a specific time frame. When was her end game or date to have lost her twenty pounds? She remembered that giving the goal a time frame increased the sense of urgency in accomplishing it (Top Achievement, n.d.).

CHAPTER ONE

Starting the role as an academic coach can be intimidating and confusing. Your first steps might be to work on developing a growth mindset. Then you will want to determine how the principal and the school leadership team view the role of academic coach for this particular school. What will you be expected to do? How can you best accomplish this? There are many issues to be considered as you move into the coaching role. Considering the specific school setting, its needs, your strengths, and the areas in which you want to grow will help you determine the specific SMART goals you should develop.

Reflect and Apply Activities

1.1. Talk to four or five individuals at your school and determine whether they have a growth or a fixed mindset. What did they say that indicated their mindset? Discuss some personal examples of how a growth mindset has or could make a difference in your life or school.

1.2. Since the role of academic or instructional coach is a new position at your school, you have been asked to work with the administrative team to help organize the instructional leadership team. Think about the individuals who work in your school. Decide who you think should be included in the instructional leadership team and why?

1.3. What SMART goals do you think Jessie should develop for her new school? Does she have enough information yet? If she doesn't, what information does she need and what should her next steps be to gather the missing information?

References

Dweck, C. S. (2006). *Mindset the new psychology of success: How we can learn to fulfill our potential.* New York: Random House.

Feiman-Nemser, S. (1996). *Teacher mentoring: A critical review.* Retrieved from http://www.ericdigests.org/1997–1/mentoring.html.

Hasbrouck, J., & Denton, C. (2005). *The reading coach: A how-to manual for success.* Longmont, CO: Sopris West.

Heick, T. (2013). *Establishing a growth mindset as a teacher: 9 statements of affirmation.* TeachThought. Retrieved from http://www.teachthought.com/teaching/establishing-growth-mindset-teacher-9-statements-affirmation/.

Lyons, C., & Pinnell, G. S. (2001). *Systems for change in literacy education: A guide to professional development.* Portsmouth, NH: Heinemann.

Merriam-Webster's collegiate dictionary (9th ed.). (1986). Coach. Springfield, MA: Merriam-Webster.

Puig, E. A., & Froelich, K. S. (2007). *The literacy coach: Guiding in the right direction.* Boston, MA: Pearson Education.

Spaulding, D. T., & Smith, G. (2012). *Instructional coaches and the instructional leadership team: A guide for school-building improvement.* Thousand Oaks, CA: Corwin.

Stephens, D., & Mills, H. (2014). Coaching as inquiry: The South Carolina reading initiative. *Reading & Writing Quarterly: Overcoming Learning Difficulties, 30*(3), 190–206.

Top Achievement. (n.d.). *Creating SMART goals.* Top Achievement Self Improvement and Personal Development Community. Retrieved from http://topachievement.com/smart.html.

Vogt., M., & Shearer, B. (2011). *Reading specialists and literacy coaches in the real world* (3rd ed.). Boston, MA: Pearson Education.

Wilson, C. (2004). Coaching and coach training in the workplace. *Industrial and Commercial Training, 36*(2/3), 96–98.

CHAPTER TWO

As she sat in the media center listening to the principal drone on, Jessie found herself daydreaming about her friends and students at the old school. She was roused from her daydream abruptly as she heard the principal say, "Let's give a round of applause for Jessie Sedlack." The principal paused as Jessie rose. "She is our new academic coach, and she is going to raise our school grade this year. Jessie, come on up here so everyone will get a chance to meet you."

What is he thinking? Jessie wondered, worrying as she rose from her seat. How should she handle this? She quickly thought about all the aspects of coaching she had read about before accepting this job. What were her options? She was going to have to get these teachers on her side. The principal obviously wanted her to feel welcome and wanted to convey that she was a valuable member of the staff. But with that comment, in his excitement, the principal had unwittingly created an "us against her" attitude. He had just made her singlehandedly responsible for raising the school grade, while leaving the teachers totally out of the picture. She could imagine what the teachers were thinking.

"Well, I am really excited to be here," Jessie responded as she reached the front of the room. "I am sure together we can raise that school grade, but I certainly will not be doing it by myself," she said with a slight laugh, attempting to lighten the atmosphere and get everyone on her side. "I am excited to be able to showcase all of your wonderful work that I have heard so much about. There is so much we can learn

CHAPTER TWO

from each other," Jessie added, emphasizing the collegiality that would be necessary for success in raising the school grade.

What in the world was the principal thinking? Jessie wondered, as she walked back to her seat. As she passed a table on the far left, she heard one voice saying, "So who does she think she is, coming in and telling us what we need to do? Doesn't she think we are already working hard with these students?" *Oh no, this is just what I was hoping to avoid,* thought Jessie. *Already they are putting up walls.* She glanced over trying to figure out who had been speaking, but it was difficult to tell since no one was talking right now. *I don't even know what I will be doing or how I can make a difference yet. Boy, do I have my work cut out for me just getting them to accept me,* she thought. *It looks like my first SMART goal will need to be developing a plan for increasing teacher buy-in with the coaching process.*

Teacher Effectiveness

What skills does Jessie need to make a difference in the school? She has been a teacher for eight years now. She taught for five years in third grade and then for three years in fifth grade. The principal had indicated that she had been chosen to fill the coaching role because she had been rated as a highly effective teacher. With the current emphasis on teacher evaluation, we hear a lot about effective teachers and highly effective teachers. So what skills make a teacher effective?

Characteristics of Effective Teachers as Determined by Teachers' Perception

Walker (2010) interviewed teachers to determine their perception of the characteristics that made effective teachers. Based on the findings from his study, he identified twelve characteristics of effective teachers. He categorized these personal and professional characteristics as (1) being prepared, (2) demonstrating a positive attitude, (3) displaying high expectations, (4) demonstrating creativity, (5) modeling fairness, (6) having a personal touch, (7) demonstrating a sense of belonging, (8) admitting mistakes, (9) having a sense of humor, (10) showing respect to students, (11) being forgiving, and (12) demonstrating compassion (p. 4). Interestingly, as you look over this list, you will notice that most of the items on the list focus on the teacher's personal characteristics and there is little emphasis on the teacher's content knowledge.

Only two of the characteristics, demonstrating a sense of belonging and showing respect to students, begin to address facets specifically related to the classroom learning environment. The final characteristic, being prepared, is specifically related to classroom instruction since it discusses teacher preparation for instruction. Only 25 percent of the characteristics seem to focus on instructional characteristics in the classroom environment.

Based on this and other research on teacher effectiveness, there seems to be a direct relationship between teachers' personal characteristics and teachers' effectiveness (Murray, Rushton & Paumonen, 1990; Stronge, 2007). Walker's (2010) list seems to support this view as well. However, research has not been able to establish that the relationship between teachers' personal characteristics and teachers' effectiveness is necessarily a causal relationship. It is not clear whether the personal characteristics enable teachers to become effective or whether effective teachers naturally develop these characteristics.

Characteristics of Effective Teachers as Determined by Student Achievement

Research has indicated that there is a relationship between teachers' skills and students' academic performance (Watson, Miller, Davis, & Cater, 2010). So perhaps identifying the characteristics of effective teachers as determined by student achievement will help to identify more of the causal characteristics. Stronge, Ward, and Grant (2011) used student achievement to compare characteristics in fifteen teacher-effectiveness dimensions between top and bottom quartile teachers as measured by student achievement. Stronge et al.'s (2011) research established that there was a strong relationship between effective teachers' characteristics and student achievement. In their research study, Stronge et al. evaluated teachers on fifteen dimensions, which were then combined to form four domains of practice: instructional delivery, student assessment, learning environment, and personal qualities.

The domain of *instructional delivery* included the elements of differentiation, learning focus, clarity, complexity, expectation of student learn-

CHAPTER TWO

ing, use of technology, and questioning. The domain of *student assessment* included assessment for understanding and providing feedback. The domain of *learning environment* included classroom management, classroom organization, and behavioral expectations. The domain of *personal qualities* included caring, positive relationships with students, fairness and respect, encouragement of responsibility, and enthusiasm. Significant differences were found between top and bottom quartile teachers in the two domains of classroom management and personal qualities. Interestingly, there were not significant differences between top and bottom quartile teachers in the domains of instructional delivery or student assessment (Watson et al., 2010). This research seems to support Walker's (2010) emphasis on the personal characteristics rather than the instructional characteristics.

Effective Coaches

But are the fifteen dimensions that Stronge et al. (2011) identified or the twelve characteristics Walker (2010) identified for teachers the same skills needed to be an effective coach? We have all known many different coaches. Not all of them were equally effective.

PBWorks's Characteristics of Effective Coaches

PBWorks (2007) created a list of six broad categories of skills that an academic coach should possess. These six categories include beliefs, teaching expertise, coaching skills, relationship skills, content expertise, and leadership skills. Stronge et al.'s (2011) list expanded on Walker's (2010) categories, but both are missing some of the important characteristics of coaches as listed by PBWorks. Neither Walker nor Stronge et al. included any aspects of adult learning or leadership skills in their list of characteristics of effective teachers. Those are two additional skill sets that effective teachers, who want to become coaches, will need to develop.

Table 2.1 compares the teacher and coaching characteristics from the research across five categories. In the Personal category, PBWorks (2007) identified specific beliefs coaches need to possess. These are similar to the beliefs teachers possess about their students, but they also include beliefs about themselves and other teachers. In the area of beliefs, coaches need

CHAPTER TWO

Table 2.1. Comparison of Research on Coaching and Teacher Characteristics across Five Categories

Category	Effective Teacher Domains (Walker, 2010)	Effective Teacher Domains (Stronge et al., 2011)	Coaching Characteristics Categories (PBWorks, 2007)
Planning/Instruction	Prepared	Instructional Delivery	Content Expertise
Assessment		Student Assessment and Feedback	Teaching Expertise
Learning Environment	Learning Environment Belonging and Respect	Learning Environment Management, Organization, and Behavior	Teaching Expertise
Personal	Personal Qualities	Personal Qualities	Beliefs, Relationship Skills
Adult Learning			Coaching Skills
Leadership			Leadership Skills

to be willing to learn, believe everyone is important and capable of growing, be passionate about growth, not assume they have "the Answer," and strive for all individuals to be the best, most effective teachers they can be.

PBWorks (2007) seems to have combined Stronge et al.'s (2011) assessment and learning environment categories into a single category they titled Teaching Expertise. Consequently this category appears in two different cells in table 2.1. According to PBWorks, coaches need to demonstrate Teaching Expertise in instructional planning, establishing classroom management and organization systems, using multiple methods of assessment and instruction easily, and being reflective practitioners. These are similar to the skills identified by Stronge et al. (2011) in the domains of the learning environment and assessment.

In the area of Adult Learning and Leadership, a category not discussed by the other two sources, PBWorks (2007) divided these two skills into two broad categories: Coaching Skills and Leadership Skills. They indicate that coaches should be skillful listeners who are able to communicate effectively, understand adult learning, diagnose teachers' needs, and provide support.

Although there are similarities between the characteristics of effective coaches and teachers, they do not require the exact same skill set. Coaches need to develop a wider variety of skill sets to be able to effectively work with adult learners. As you look over the list of identified characteristics, it becomes evident that just being an effective teacher does not provide all of the skills necessary to be an effective coach.

Coaching and Supervision

Sometimes coaching is perceived as supervision, as was evident by the teacher's comment Jessie overhead in the scenario at the beginning of this chapter. However, coaching is not supervision. The term "supervision" relates to being judged and evaluated by a supervisor. A supervisory relationship is a mandatory relationship. Even though you might have a great relationship with your supervisor, it is still someone to whom you report. You do not get to pick your supervisor, no matter how much you may wish you could at times. A supervisory relationship is unsolicited. Carter (2003) explained the distinction between coaching and supervision by indicating that supervising has a "focus on upholding standards and managing resources" (p. 20), but coaching focuses on individuals as learners, who are working on using their strengths to achieve their specific, desired goals.

Think about the list of characteristics below. Which of the following phrases best describe coaching and which phrases best describe supervision? Take a minute to divide the list into the two groups.

Evaluating Performance	Invited
Judging Teachers	Peer to Peer
Reported	Voluntary
Confidential	Professional Competence
Unsolicited	Solicited
Knowledgeable	Corrective Measures

Coaching Is Not Supervision

This list of characteristics could possibly be divided as illustrated in table 2.2. You will notice that some characteristics seem to belong in both columns, which further illustrates some of the similarities between the coaching and the supervision roles. However, some characteristics seem to fit more specifically in one area or the other.

Table 2.2. Comparison of Coaching and Supervision Characteristics

Coaching	Supervision
Invited	Evaluating Performance
Peer to Peer	Judging Teachers
Voluntary	Reported
Knowledgeable	Knowledgeable
Focused on Student Growth	Corrective Measures
Confidential	Upholding Standards
Solicited	Unsolicited

Coaching is about providing support rather than evaluating (Hasbrouck & Denton, 2005). The following five statements illustrate important aspects of the coaching process:

1. Coaching is built on trust and confidence.

2. Coaching is not about making evaluative decisions related to professional competence.

3. Coaching is a voluntary, peer-to-peer process.

4. Coaching is about the well-being of students, not judging or evaluating teachers.

5. Coaching is about being invited to observe a lesson or instructional practice and providing feedback (p. 24).

Components of Coaching

The Literacy Coach Clearinghouse (2009) is a wonderful resource that identifies coaching and leadership skills and resources that can help coaches be successful. Their *Self-Assessment for Elementary Literacy Coaches* is divided into ten categories. An analysis of these categories can help current or potential coaches determine their strengths and areas for growth in each category: foundations of literacy, assessment, content area instruction, writing, differentiated instruction, classroom coaching, facilitating adult learning, building capacity within the school, and working within a broader school reform context (p. 3–21).

CHAPTER TWO

Relationship Skills

In classroom or one-to-one coaching, relationship skills are particularly important (PBWorks, 2007; Literacy Coach Clearinghouse, 2009). These relationships skills require coaches to be able to demonstrate trust by respecting others and being an integral part of a team of teachers and administrators. All team members must be able to work well together to achieve the established school goals.

Leadership Skills

The leadership skills, as identified by PBWorks (2007), include the ability to analyze data, plan for improvement, communicate the school vision, and align with school goals. The Literacy Coach Clearinghouse (2009) expands on these leadership skills by dividing them into two categories: building capacity within the school, and working within a broader school-reform context. These categories encompass establishing the school-wide literacy team, developing a literacy plan, determining important elements, monitoring progress, communicating with stakeholders, coordinating school and classroom efforts, mentoring and coaching for success, integrating technology, addressing barriers, building community partnerships, and coordinating school reform (Literacy Coach Clearinghouse, 2009, p. 18–21).

Content Area Skills

The Literacy Coach Clearinghouse also more extensively develops the content area knowledge that is not discussed by either Walker (2010) or Stronge et al. (2011). The Literacy Coach Clearinghouse delineates the importance of knowing the content area standards, understanding cognitive strategies, analyzing and selecting appropriate content area texts and media, implementing effective instructional practices, and developing methods for increasing student engagement.

Literacy Skills

Although the Literacy Coach self-assessment tool is specifically written for literacy coaches, coaches in any area would profit from expanding their understanding of literacy. Students need well-developed literacy skills to understand the content area texts. Whether the academic coach is a science, social studies, or math coach, the coach needs to understand literacy. If students cannot read the content, they will not successfully master it. Academic coaches should be familiar with literacy components such as understanding the six strands of literacy (oral language, phonemic awareness, phonics, vocabulary, fluency, and comprehension) and the skills within each of these strands (Florida Department of Education, 2011, p. 15).

Assessment Skills

Also important is the coach's understanding of the assessment system used by the school, including norm- and criterion-referenced assessments; formative, screening, authentic, and informal assessments, the data these assessments provide, and how the data can be used to identify and direct instruction to meet students' academic needs.

Writing Skills

A knowledge and understanding of the writing process is an often overlooked component for content area coaches; however, students need to be able to use writing to express their understanding in any content area. The knowledge about writing that coaches should possess would include an understanding of writing skills, writing methods for various genres, writing revision, mechanics, organization, voice, grammar, spelling, capitalization, punctuation, increasing student engagement, and using technology.

Differentiation Skills

Another important skill for all coaches would be the ability to differentiate instruction. If coaches do not possess this skill, they will not be able to support teachers as they attempt to differentiate for their students. Coaches need to be able to help teachers differentiate in at least four different elements: content, process, product, and the learning environment (Tomlinson, 2004).

Differentiating in content requires the ability to adapt the content by changing either what the student needs to learn or the way in which he will obtain access to the information. This can be accomplished by offering materials at various readability levels, using recorded materials, incorporating buddy reading, or adding additional visual support. To differentiate by process, teachers can vary the activities in which the student engages. Some options teachers could consider incorporating would be tiered activities, interest centers, personal agendas, manipulatives, or various lengths of time to complete activities (Tomlinson, 2004).

Differentiation by product occurs when teachers provide various ways that the student can demonstrate her learning through different media, such as writing, speaking, drawing, or drama. Differentiating the amount of support could be provided during the completion of the activity. Products could be completed individually, in pairs, or in small groups depending on student needs (Tomlinson, 2004).

Finally, differentiation in the learning environment would include making sure that within the classroom environment routines and guidelines are clear, sections of the room free from distractions are provided, and various cultures and home settings are supported. Through these types of differentiation, various reading materials, flexible groups, and learning styles are supported. With classroom populations becoming increasingly diverse academically, culturally, socioeconomically, and linguistically, the teacher's ability to differentiate has become an increasingly important skill (Tomlinson, 2004).

Adult Learning Skills

The Literacy Coach Clearinghouse (2009) included the category of facilitating adult learning that PBWorks (2007) did not identify. The Literacy Coach Clearinghouse indicated that the coach should understand how to support teachers at different stages in their careers and how to identify teacher strengths. Coaches need to be able to facilitate change, support adult learners, lead groups, and provide targeted instructional practices. These are all important activities, but coaches need to understand that just like students, not all teachers have the same needs at the same time. Determining the appropriate support to provide for each teacher can be a challenging situation.

Reflect and Apply Activities

2.1. Based on the information in this chapter and your personal experience, construct a Venn diagram comparing the characteristics of effective teachers and coaches. Make sure to include any characteristics you feel are important but were not previously discussed.

2.2. Analyze the best or worst experience you have had being coached or providing coaching. This may be academic coaching or coaching in any other area. Explain what parts of this were particularly helpful and what parts could have been improved. What skills were strong and what skills need to be further developed?

2.3. Talk to your coworkers and generate a list of areas in which teachers would like to expand their knowledge. How does this list compare to the list generated by the Literacy Coach Clearinghouse?

References

Carter, M. (2003). Supervising or coaching—What's the difference? *Child Care Information Exchange*, 20–22. Redmond, WA. Retrieved from http://cocoaches.net/uploads/Supervising_or_Coaching.pdf.

Florida Department of Education. (2011). *State literacy plan*. Retrieved from http://www.justreadflorida.com/pdf/StrivingReaders.pdf.

Hasbrouck, J., & Denton, C. (2005). *The reading coach: A how-to manual for success*. Longmont, CO: Sopris West.

Literacy Coach Clearinghouse. (2009). *Self-assessment for elementary literacy coaches*. Retrieved from http://www.literacycoachingonline.org/briefs/tools/self_assessment_for_elem_lit_coaches.pdf.

Murray, H. G., Rushton, J. P., & Paunonen, S. V. (1990). Teacher personality traits and student instructional ratings in six types of university courses. *Journal of Educational Psychology*, 82, 250–61. doi: 10,1037/0022-0663,82,2,250.

PBWorks. (2007). *Becoming an effective coach*. Retrieved from http://coaches.pbworks.com/w/page/7518652/Becoming%20an%20Effective%20Coach#CharacteristicsofEffectiveCoaches.

CHAPTER TWO

Stronge, J. H. (2007). *Qualities of effective teachers.* Alexandria, VA: Association for Supervision and Curriculum Development.

Stronge, J. H., Ward, T. J., & Grant, L. W. (2011). What makes good teachers good? A cross-case analysis of the connection between teacher effectiveness and student achievement. *Journal of Teacher Education, 62*(4), 339–55.

Tomlinson, C. A. (2004). *Differentiation of instruction in the elementary grades.* Retrieved from http://www.ericdigests.org/2001-2/elementary.html.

Walker, R. J. (2010). *12 characteristics of an effective teacher: A longitudinal retrospective qualitative quasi-research study of in-service and pre-service teachers' opinions of the characteristics of an effective teacher.* Retrieved from http://files.eric.ed.gov/fulltext/ED509938.pdf.

Watson, S., Miller, T., Davis, L., & Carter, P. (2010). Teachers' perceptions of the effective teacher. *Research in the Schools, 17*(2), 11–22.

CHAPTER THREE

Jessie stuck her head through the principal's door.

"Hi," she said. "Are you ready for me, or should I come back later? You look really busy."

"I was just doing some research on the factors that impact learning," he replied, looking up from his computer. "I found some interesting information about factors that impact long- and short-term memory. I wonder how many of our teachers consider these when they are constructing lessons," he mused. "I hear a lot of complaints about students not remembering what teachers are teaching."

"Well, all the teachers have an education background, so they probably use it," Jessie observed.

"Researchers have made some really interesting discoveries about learning and the way we process information in the last few years, so unless they recently graduated, they might not know it. Then there are the teachers we have who are coming from another career. They probably did not take any education courses," the principal continued. "Not all teachers are at the same stage in their career, and they don't all know or need the same thing."

"I really hadn't thought about those people who are career changers," Jessie observed. "Do we have a lot of second-career teachers in our building?"

"Actually, between a quarter and a half of them are in their second career. You might be in a great position to share this information about learning and memory with the staff—not just in telling them the facts, but

CHAPTER THREE

through the way you structure professional development, you can model the strategies. You would, of course, have to explain why you structured the professional development the way you did, but modeling would be a great first step.

"Why don't you watch some professional development videos and make a list of the factors that impact learning that the presenters considered and those that they didn't? Think about why some of the presentations were more effective than others. Then let's talk about it the next time we meet. I would like to end up with a list of some of the factors that impact learning that we want the staff to consider when constructing their lessons."

Jessie walked out of her weekly meeting with the principal mulling over the discussion. He had given her a lot to think about. Watching teaching videos would be a great way to start.

Categories of Teachers

The principal got Jessie thinking about teachers having differing needs. Where teachers are in their career and their previous experiences are important factors that can impact their professional development needs and their attitude toward teaching, the coach, and students. Hasbrouck and Denton (2005) divided teachers into four groups: eager and open, eager but resistant, reluctant but not resistant, and reluctant and resistant (p. 25).

Beginning teachers tend to be in the eager and open category (Hasbrouck & Denton, 2005). They generally appreciate any support that is provided as they are developing their instructional practices. But not all teachers are in this first category of being eager and open. Eager but resistant teachers are those who want to see changes in their students, but often feel that the problems they are experiencing are caused by factors outside of their control, whether it is the parents, the students, previous teachers, or the educational system. Reluctant but not resistant teachers would be those who are typically successful teachers and don't feel a need for additional support. The teacher Jessie overheard talking in the beginning of the last chapter would fit into the reluctant and resistant group. The teacher did not think that the academic coach could help her in any way. Sometimes these teachers are resistant to making changes, and sometimes they have worked in a closed-door environment for so long that they are nervous about having another adult in their classroom. Learning to determine where teachers are in their career and their receptiveness toward coaching will be an important step in helping the coach know how to approach each teacher and what kind of support to offer.

Processing Information

As the academic coach, you will be working with teachers and asking them to process new information and then apply it in their classroom with their students. How does this happen and how can we increase the likelihood of it occurring? In order to do this effectively, you need to understand how the brain processes and uses information.

The human brain is not a computer; it is so much more! Computers are very effective for processing information; however, effective teaching requires more than just processing the information. Teaching involves analyzing and synthesizing the information gained from the content knowledge and classroom environment and then making judgments about that information. The research about learning seems to indicate that learners will gain greater understanding and pleasure from learning when they are allowed to transfer the learning into a new creative format or situation (Sousa, 2011).

Short-Term Memory

As a coach, it is your job to help teachers at different stages in their careers understand new information. A better understanding of the steps involved in processing information will help you to present information in a way that is more likely to result in learners being able to transfer and apply concepts.

Although we often don't think about the role our senses play in the learning process, learning begins with the senses. All five senses, although constantly providing information, do not contribute information equally. Throughout our lifetime, our senses of sight, hearing, and touch provide us with the most information, more than smelling and tasting do. The senses of taste and smell, although important, do not seem to have as great an impact on learning.

In order for the information from your senses to be processed, the information first needs to enter the short-term memory, which is composed

CHAPTER THREE

of two areas: immediate memory and working memory. Immediate memory holds onto information from your senses for about thirty seconds, or approximately long enough to enter an e-mail address or an event into your phone (Sousa, 2011).

Working Memory

Working memory is the temporary storage place where conscious processing occurs. The information in working memory can be either information you just received from your senses or information that you retrieve from what you have already stored in long-term memory. "Working memory is often thought of as a mental workspace we can use to store important information in the course of mental activities" (Gathercole & Alloway, 2007, p. 4). Working memory, however, does not have just one physical location in the brain; instead, several parts of the brain work together (Malamed, 2015).

Working memory has a three-part system: the central control mechanism, the phonological loop, and the visuospatial sketchpad. In the brain, the central control mechanism combines and processes the information provided by the phonological loop (the auditory signals) and the visuospatial sketchpad (the visual and spatial information). The importance of understanding working memory for teaching is that combining information from both parts in the central control mechanism strengthens the messages the brain receives. The combination of auditory and visual rehearsing during instruction increases the working memory's interaction with long-term memory and increases the probability that the information will be retained (Sousa, 2011).

The amount of information that can be stored in working memory is limited. The number of chunks of information that can be retained is impacted by interest, delay, and distractions. The amount of information that can be held in working memory decreases as the number of distractions, information, and mental demands increases. However, generally, adults can retain about three to five chunks of information in working memory for about ten to twenty minutes until they become fatigued or bored and their focus shifts to other ideas. For learners to remain focused longer than that, they must change the way they are working with the concepts. This shift does not need to be major; it can be as simple as moving from thinking about the information to applying it in a new situation (Sousa, 2011).

Increasing Working Memory

When learners believe they will be accountable for the information, the amount of processing time increases. In addition, when prompt, specific, and corrective feedback is provided, learners are more likely to be able to continue processing information for a longer period of time. In education we often discuss the role of formative assessments for the teacher. However, formative assessments during instruction are particularly helpful for the learner as well. They provide feedback and increase the learner's attention to the concepts or information being presented (Sousa, 2011).

Hunter (2004) identified the level of concern as an important factor in motivation and retention. He found that helpful anxiety, such as being concerned about your job performance, was a factor that increased learning. But when there was either too much concern or anxiety or no concern at all, the learning process stopped.

Long-Term Memory

These ideas have important implications for structuring professional development. The principal had asked Jessie to evaluate the learning principles used in the professional development videos she watched. Jessie noticed that dividing the session into two fifteen- to twenty-minute components, for example, was more effective than one forty-minute session. She found it easier to remember the information presented. After reading about learning theory and watching numerous professional development videos, Jessie composed a checklist she could use to evaluate the professional development sessions she watched and later those she presented.

Jessie created the Short-Term Memory Checklist in appendix A. She divided the information into three categories: presentation, environmental, and learner characteristics. On the checklist she evaluated characteristics like the number of chunks of information, the length of time the information was kept in short-term memory, the formative assessments used, the level of concern, the learner's accountability for the information, and the amount of distractions.

CHAPTER THREE

Moving Information from Short-Term to Long-Term Memory

The determination of whether information should be moved to long-term memory is based on responses to two questions: Does the information make sense? And does it have meaning? The teacher's job is to help the learner make meaning. Meaning can be created in a number of different ways. Meaning can be accomplished through modeling or by relating the topic to previous experiences. At other times, artificial meaning can be created through the use of mnemonic devices. However, not all information that is processed in short-term memory is retained. As the learner attempts to move information from working (short-term) to long-term memory, that greatest loss of information will occur within the first twenty-four hours (Sousa, 2011).

For retention of information to occur, it is important for the learner to create schemata in their long-term memory. This is done by categorizing and grouping the specific topics and pieces of information to be learned. There are two types of schemata: general and specific. As the student is learning new knowledge, this information processes through the short-term memory into the long-term memory with the ultimate goal being that the newly learned knowledge goes into the appropriate schema in the long-term memory. Your schema is like a file folder, and your long-term memory is like a large filing cabinet with unlimited capacity.

It is important that the correct information goes into the appropriate folder; otherwise, you won't be able to immediately retrieve the desired information. Immediate retrieval of information is the main goal of filing concepts, ideas, or experiences in long-term memory. If the information is not filed correctly, the person experiences "tip of the tongue" syndrome. You know the information is filed in your long-term memory; however, you cannot seem to find it. You know the answer is there and it is on the "tip of your tongue," but you just can't quite seem to remember it. You might end up retrieving the information much later, when it is not needed. Even though you aren't consciously thinking about it, the brain continues to look for the answer until it is found. That is why you remember the information hours later when it seems to "pop" into your head. The brain has completed the task of retrieving the requested information, albeit hours later and when the information is not needed.

Self-Concept

Self-concept can also have a significant impact on retention and learning. Our belief system is formed by all of the information in our long-term storage areas. These experiences and information help us to understand and make sense of events and the world. Our self-concept is part of this belief system. Past positive or negative experiences can enhance or block our ability to process new information. If a learner has had a negative experience with this information in the past (for example, data analysis), he will tend to struggle with the information the next time he encounters it.

Humor

The use of humor can also enhance retention of information. Sousa (2011) described the physiological and psychological benefits of humor. In the physiological area, humor and laughing provide more oxygen to fuel the brain. This causes an endorphin surge; decreases stress, pain, and blood pressure; and boosts immune defenses. There are psychological benefits for both the teacher and the learner. Humor helps the teacher increase attention and creates a positive learning climate. Humor benefits the learner by increasing retention and recall and improving mental health. For these reasons, humor provides an effective discipline tool for sustaining and refocusing attention and engagement.

Teaching Implications

As we apply the concepts about coaching, the brain, and learning to situations in working with teachers, there are some important points to remember. Learners need support, acceptance, and adequate time for processing and reflection. Modeling is an important process in any learning situation: it helps the learner to visualize how they could respond in various situations. Because of the constraints of working memory and attention, learners need opportunities to move, discuss, and explain information to others.

Movement is important for teachers as well. Movement around the room can allow teachers to use proximity to help learners stay on task. Because of limits to attention, teachers should plan to use a variety of ways to

CHAPTER THREE

group or pair learners to keep them actively involved in the learning process. In addition, teachers need to provide time for processing and reflection, which help to increase accountability. Clarifying any learner misunderstandings is an important component of any instruction (Sousa, 2011).

Jessie's checklist for evaluating instruction is found in appendix A.

Reflect and Apply Activities

3.1. Take the Literacy Coach self-assessment found at http://www.literacycoachingonline.org/briefs/tools/self_assessment_for_elem_lit_coaches.pdf. Develop a SMART goal to address one area where you would like to expand your skills. Make sure it contains all the components of a SMART goal.

3.2. Identify at least one teacher on your school staff that you think typifies each of the teacher categories: eager and open, eager but resistant, reluctant but not resistant, and reluctant and resistant. Develop a plan for building a relationship with each of these four teachers. Because they are at different stages in their careers, the first steps might need to be significantly different.

3.3. Analyze a professional development presentation you attended or watched online using appendix A. How was information structured to incorporate the concepts of short-term memory, humor, and self-concept? If you don't think these were addressed effectively, how could the professional development have been revised to better address these concepts?

References

Gathercole, S. E., & Alloway, T. P. (2007). *Understanding working memory: A classroom guide*. London: Harcourt Assessment. Retrieved from http://www.york.ac.uk/res/wml/Classroom%20guide.pdf.

Hasbrouck, J., & Denton, C. (2005). *The reading coach: A how-to manual for success*. Longmont, CO: Sopris West.

Hunter, M. (2004). *Mastery teaching*. Thousand Oaks, CA: Corwin.

CHAPTER THREE

Literacy Coach Clearinghouse. (2009). *Self-assessment of elementary literacy coaches*. Retrieved from http://www.literacycoachingonline.org/briefs/tools/self_assessment_for_elem_lit_coaches.pdf.

Malamed, C. (2015). 20 facts you must know about working memory. *The eLearning Coach*. Retrieved from http://theelearningcoach.com/learning/20-facts-about-working-memory/.

Sousa, D. A. (2011). *How the brain learns* (4th ed.). Thousand Oaks, CA: Corwin.

CHAPTER FOUR

Boy, this first week has really been hectic, Jessie thought as she drove to the coaches' meeting at the district office. *I would not have thought I could have put in so much time and still feel so far behind. This coaching job is making my days as a teacher seem like a piece of cake. I hit my office an hour before school starts, and I am still going strong long after the teachers have left. But on the positive side, I feel like I am starting to recognize most of the staff. I can put a name with the faces when I pass them in the hall, and I know what most of them are teaching. No one has reached out to me as a coach yet, but the principal is sure keeping me busy.*

The school's instructional team met last week, and we worked on developing a job description. Well, based on the job description, I certainly won't be bored, she thought with a sigh. *I am supposed to meet with each grade-level team each week, lead book studies, provide professional development, model lessons, work with teachers, and analyze data—just for starters. Some of those things seem straightforward and are things I have done before. But some of them I am really lost on, which is why I was especially excited to see the e-mail with the agenda for today's coaches' meeting at the district offices. There are three topics on the agenda, and I need all of them! We are going to be talking about the characteristics of a good coach, data analysis, and the coaching cycle.*

Jessie pulled into a parking space in front of the district office, anxious to meet the rest of the coaches. As she walked through the door, she saw a small group gathered around the Keurig and wandered over.

"Hi, I'm Jessie," she said, reaching for a cup.

CHAPTER FOUR

"Great to meet you. This is Tom, and Marilyn, and I am Kathryn. Right now the district has hired only four coaches, but that is double what we had last year," Kathryn added with a smile. "Tom and I started working as coaches last year," she continued by way of explanation. "Grab your cup of coffee and bring it over to the table. We are going to start the meeting with a general discussion about the characteristics that make a good coach. Then we are going to move into a discussion of school data. I have a copy of the data from each of the schools on the table. Take a seat in front of your school's data so that we will be ready to begin discussing different ways to analyze that data."

"Great," Jessie replied. "Analyzing school data is a topic I really need. Up to this point I have just been given the data for my class and been expected to work with my students to correct any areas of deficit. But I have no idea what to do with the data from the entire school."

"Well, I'm glad we are going to be discussing it, then," Kathryn commented. "Data analysis is actually the starting point of the whole coaching cycle. Later today we will be examining the four components of the coaching cycle. Remember that all coaching does not look the same. It can occur in many different ways."

Leadership Characteristics

MIWorks (n.d.) created a leadership survey that provides some insight into the important characteristics for content area academic coaches. Although written as individual statements, the twenty statements in the survey could be grouped into five categories: personal characteristics, interpersonal characteristics, managerial skills, communication style, and data analysis and interpretation (p. 1). The statements duplicate many of the ideas presented in the Literacy Coach Clearinghouse self-assessment tool (2009).

Comparing Characteristics of Effective Coaches

Many different sources provide information about characteristics of effective coaches. The coaching categories identified by three of those sources are compared in table 4.1. The table compares the coaching characteristics identified by the Literacy Coach self-assessment (2009), the PBWorks (2007) characteristics that we discussed in chapter 2, and the

CHAPTER FOUR

Table 4.1. Coaching and Leadership Characteristics Identified by Source

Category	Self-Assessment (Literacy Coach Clearinghouse, 2009)	Coaching Characteristics (PBWorks, 2007)	Leadership Survey (MIWorks, n.d.)
Instructional Practices	Foundations of Literacy	Teaching Expertise	
Assessment	Assessment		Data Analysis
Content Area Instruction	Content Area Instruction	Content Expertise	
Writing	Writing		
Differentiation	Differentiated Instruction		
Classroom and Teacher Relationships	Classroom Coaching	Relationship Skills	Interpersonal Communication
Adult Learning	Facilitating Adult Learning	Beliefs	Personal
Building School Capacity	Building School Capacity	Leadership Skills	Managerial
Broader School Reform	Broader School Reform		

characteristics listed in the MIWorks leadership survey (n.d.). Although there is some overlap, not every category was addressed by each source. The Literacy Coach Clearinghouse (2009) self-assessment contained the most extensive list of coaching characteristics. In fact, three areas—writing, differentiated instruction, and broad school reform—were identified only by the Literacy Coach Clearinghouse. Although the assessment category was included in two of the sources, the emphasis addressed in each was different. The Literacy Coach Clearinghouse (2009) self-assessment focused on coaches being able to identify and use appropriate assessments, while MIWorks (n.d.) focused on the disaggregation and analysis of the data the assessments provided. Data analysis is an area where MIWorks's leadership survey identified additional characteristics that were not addressed by either of the other two sources.

Data Analysis

With the increased emphasis on the use of data to meet standards and improve school performance, the ability to analyze data has taken on a more significant role in the coach's daily responsibilities. Data comes in many forms and from many different sources at the district, school, classroom, or individual student level. This data could be the quantitative results from summative high-stakes assessments, report cards, student behavior, school attendance, or classroom assessments, just to name a few areas. However, the data could also be qualitative in nature and come from teachers, administrators, parents, or the community. All of these sources can provide the coach with important information to help guide instruction.

Consequently, the coach needs to be able to analyze and determine patterns and areas of concern so that the data can be used to direct and improve instructional effectiveness. However, data can be examined in many different ways. At the classroom level, data can be used to provide information about specific students' needs. Data can also be used at the whole-school level to provide information about the entire school or it can be disaggregated and used to provide information about various subgroups within the school (Spaulding & Smith, 2012).

Disaggregation

Data needs to be disaggregated to better understand patterns within the data. This is what Jessie was going to learn how to do in her meeting. *Disaggregation* is examining the data to determine whether a difference exists in performance between two subgroups based on one or more variables (Spaulding & Smith, 2012). These variations could be differences in performance between grade levels, racial groups, gender, and so forth. As the data is analyzed, the analysis sometimes creates more questions than answers. Therefore, the result of the analysis may be a need to drill down further into the data and analyze the data using another analytical method. These methods of disaggregation might include trend, cohort, or longitudinal analysis.

Trend

Trend analysis can provide important information about specific groups or time periods. This analysis can be used to determine patterns in student performance at the same grade level or over a certain number of years (Spaulding & Smith, 2012). For example, you might be interested in knowing whether seventh graders experience difficulty with the same standards each year. If, for a number of years in a row, seventh graders consistently answer the questions about percentages on the state assessment incorrectly, then this would indicate that the seventh-grade math teachers might want to examine the instruction and standards that are being addressed in the unit on percentages. They would want to see whether the standards on the assessments are being assessed in the same way that they are being taught. If they are being assessed in the same way, it would be important to ascertain whether there is a more effective way to teach these particular standards. A trend analysis can provide important information about instructional practices and their match with assessment.

Cohort

Cohort analysis examines the data for a specific group or cohort of students. This could be the data from one assessment, or it could be data over several years. You might be interested in knowing whether this particular group of sixth graders made about the same amount of progress in fifth grade as they did in sixth grade. If 60 percent of the students earned a passing score on the state assessment in fifth grade but only 30 percent earned a passing score in sixth grade, then we would want to know what caused the difference between these two years.

We all know, having worked with multiple groups of students, that the characteristics of each group are not the same. Although you might be teaching the same content, some groups seem to grasp it more quickly than others. At other times, some groups of students seem to progress more quickly using one instructional method as compared to another instructional method.

It would be important to know the progress of one particular group or cohort of students. You might want to know whether Ms. Smith's fifth-grade class experienced about the same amount of growth as Mr. Jones's fifth-grade class. To determine that information, you would want to do a cohort analysis. In addition, a cohort analysis could be used, for example, to determine whether male students show the same level of growth as female students or whether low-socioeconomic-status (SES) students show the same level of growth as middle-income students. A cohort analysis can be used to help you to compare the progress of various subgroups within the school.

Longitudinal

A *longitudinal analysis* examines a cohort of students over a longer period of time. You may want to examine the growth pattern of a specific group of fifth-grade students on their state assessment since kindergarten. A longitudinal analysis would allow you to examine how much growth has occurred each year. This would help you to determine whether the instruction that occurred this year impacted their growth more positively or negatively than previous instruction. If there was a greater positive growth than in other years, you would want to attempt to identify what was done differently so that the same rate of positive academic growth continues next year (Spaulding & Smith, 2012).

Data Provides the Basis for the Coaching Process

Data analysis becomes the basis for the coaching process. The analysis can be used to identify potential concerns related to student growth. In order to increase student growth, professional development is provided to expand teachers' instructional practices in the specific identified area.

There are various different models that are used to illustrate the coaching process. Depending on which model you examine, there might be four or five steps in the coaching cycle. However, each of the models begins by identifying the area of need. (1) Data analysis provides a way to identify that need, so it is the first step. (2) After the need is identified, the goal is set. (The five-step models tend to separate the goal setting from the data analysis, while the four-step models combine steps 1 and 2 in a single process.) (3) The goal area is investigated in the literature to determine instructional practices that could be used to address the area of concern. (4) Based upon the information from the literature, a professional plan is developed. The coach then works with teachers to address their identified areas of need. There are many possible activities that could be included in this portion of the cycle. Some of the coaching activities could include providing opportunities for the teacher to observe other teachers and groups of students, modeling techniques and instructional strategies, encouraging teachers to participate in professional learning communities (PLCs), conducting workshops, advising and supporting teachers, organizing and managing the curricular instruction, locating instructional

CHAPTER FOUR

materials, conducting action research, and facilitating professional development. (5) The final step in the coaching process would be to reexamine the data and compare it to any progress-monitoring data that has been collected in an attempt to reflect upon and determine whether the newly instituted practices were effective in meeting the students' needs. Then the cycle begins again, leading to a further refinement of the instructional practices.

Professional Development

The coaching cycle supports learning and professional development, but that professional development can take many different forms. For coaches to provide effective instruction and support, whether it occurs one-on-one, in a small group, or in a large group, they need to understand the learning and retention process while providing adult learners an opportunity to be active participants who have control over their own learning.

Adult Learners

Adult learners tend to choose to learn what is currently applicable to their environment. Hence, adult learners need to understand why the knowledge you are providing is important to them before you begin the professional development. If you do not have this dialogue with your group before your presentation, they may not realize the importance of your information until it is too late. If this happens, they may not begin listening to your presentation until it is halfway over. You need to state up front not only why the information you are presenting is applicable to the teachers' current instructional environment but also how it will help them become better educators. Once you do this, you will have their attention from the beginning of the presentation. By starting the presentation with this explanation, your adult learners will become more astute listeners and learners.

Learning Improves Our Brain

Learning changes and improves our brain. It does not increase the number of brain cells within our brain, but instead it increases blood flow to the brain allowing for more activity regarding the firing of neuro synapses and increasing the number of branches and connections those cells have. Our experiences and what we learn create memories. Those memories are not stored as a single unit; instead, various portions are categorized and stored in different areas throughout the brain. The greater the number of connections to an experience, idea, or concept, the more likely the information will be stored in different networks within the brain. This gives the learner more opportunities to retrieve the new information and makes the information more useful (Sousa, 2011).

Long-Term Memory

Our goal in instruction is move information from short-term to long-term memory. We discussed short-term memory in chapter 3. We are going to examine long-term memory in more depth here.

Information enters your short-term memory and then is moved to long-term memory. Short-term memory is like placing information in a file folder and long-term memory is like a large filing cabinet with unlimited capacity. Schemata are created when the information leaves the short-term memory and enters the long-term memory. As you move information into long-term memory, you subconsciously determine whether this information is "general" or "specific." For example, a lecture on automobiles will create a "general schema" about cars, whereas a lecture on Chevrolets will create a "specific schema" and place this specific information on Chevrolets in the established general schema for automobiles. You can have many specific schemata in one general schema. The more specific schemata one has in their general schema, the faster the retrieval rate of the cognitive information. The main constraint on recall is not the capacity of long-term memory but the accessibility of the information in long-term memory.

Types of Long-Term Memory

There is some disagreement about the number of types of long-term memory. Tulving (1972) proposed three different types of long-term memory: procedural, semantic, and episodic; while Sousa (2011) divided long-term memory into two types: declarative and nondeclarative.

Declarative Memory

Cohen and Squire (1980) describe declarative memory as knowing specific information about something. Declarative memory, or conscious or explicit memory, includes the memory of names, facts, music, and objects. Sousa's (2011) declarative memory can be divided into Tulving's (1972) two types of memory: episodic and semantic.

Episodic memory is the conscious memory of events in your life, such as your college graduation or your first date. Semantic memory encompasses information about the world, word meanings, and general knowledge (Sousa, 2011). These would include the isolated bits of facts and data that you know, such as the name of the first president of the United States or the causes of the Revolutionary War. These semantic memories are not necessarily related to a specific event in your life.

Nondeclarative Memory

Nondeclarative or implicit memory includes those things not tied to a specific event, such as brushing your teeth. There are four types of nondeclarative memories stored in this portion of your brain: procedural, perceptual representation system, classical conditioning, and nonassociative learning.

Cohen and Squire (1980) describe procedural memory as knowing how to do something. This knowledge would include learned motor or cognitive skills such as tying your shoes or long division. Typically these memories are automatic and unconscious.

The perceptual representation memory system encompasses the structure and form of words prompted by prior experiences but without specific recall of an event or process. This memory system would include our ability for visual closure in shapes, words, or phrases. When part of a word or picture is hidden, you are capable of determining the part that is not showing.

Classical conditioning memory occurs when a conditioned stimulus results in a conditioned response. This memory system would include learning by association (Sousa, 2011). The meaning of the fire alarm would be a good example of this type of learning. When the fire alarm goes off, we are conditioned to quickly leave the building.

Nonassociative memories would include those stimuli to which we have learned not to respond. The ticking of the clock or the humming of

CHAPTER FOUR

the refrigerator would be examples of this type of nondeclarative memories.

There are many different types of long-term memories that are filed in different ways within the brain.

Application

Effective coaches demonstrate many different characteristics. One of these is the ability to analyze data. Data analysis can occur in many different ways, but this analysis helps to identify the needs that provide the basis for the coaching cycle. Coaching is then provided to address the identified needs. The goal of coaching is to move information from short-term to long-term memory. This can sometimes be a challenge because there are so many different types of memories that need to be filed in ways that allow them to be retrieved. An understanding of the long- and short-term memory processes makes it easier for the coach to construct lessons that facilitate this transfer. When coaching is provided, it needs to facilitate the movement of information from short- to long-term memory.

Reflect and Apply Activities

4.1. Based on the information in this chapter, table 4.1, and your personal experience, construct a Venn diagram comparing the characteristics of effective coaches and leaders. Make sure to include any characteristics you feel are important but were not previously discussed.

4.2. Examine your school's assessment data. Determine the cohorts on which you record data. Various states record data in different ways, but typically data needs to be disaggregated by subgroups. Identify the subgroups where the data from your school indicates concerns.

4.3. As the coach, you will need to assist your teachers in conveying both declarative and nondeclarative information. Classify the concepts that teachers in your school teach that would fit into each category.

References

Cohen, N. J., & Squire, L. R. (1980). Preserved learning and retention of pattern analyzing skills in amnesia: Dissociation of knowing how and knowing that. *Science, 210,* 207–9.

Literacy Coach Clearinghouse. (2009). *Self-assessment of elementary literacy coaches.* Retrieved from http://www.literacycoachingonline.org/briefs/tools/self_assessment_for_elem_lit_coaches.pdf.

MIWorks.org. (n.d.). *Leadership self-assessment.* Retrieved from http://miworks.org/virtualcareerlab/Effective%20Leadership/Leadership%20Self%20Assessment.pdf.

PBWorks. (2007). *Becoming an effective coach.* Retrieved from http://coaches.pbworks.com/w/page/7518652/Becoming%20an%20Effective%20Coach#CharacteristicsofEffectiveCoaches.

Sousa, D. A. (2011). *How the brain learns* (4th ed.). Thousand Oaks, CA: Corwin.

Spaulding, D. T., & Smith, G. (2012). *Instructional coaches and the instructional leadership team: A guide for school-building improvement.* Thousand Oaks, CA: Corwin.

Tulving, E. (1972). Episodic and semantic memory. In E. Tulving & W. Donaldson (Eds.), *Organization of Memory,* 381–403. New York: Academic Press.

CHAPTER FIVE

Time is really flying by, Jessie thought as she headed toward her third meeting with the principal. She had been at Smith almost a month now. She was really excited about the checklist she had brought to share with the principal. Hopefully it would be a good starting point for their discussion on working with the teachers about concepts related to learning.

"Hi," Jessie said as she sat down at the table after being invited into the principal's office. "How have things been going?"

"Things are great here. Are you starting to feel settled?" the principal asked.

"Yes, and I am really excited about all I have learned this last week. I have watched numerous videos, and I feel like I am really starting to see a lot of issues related to short-term memory and instruction," Jessie responded. "It has really been an interesting activity."

"That's wonderful," he said. "I am glad you found it enlightening."

"I have brought the list I started to show you where I am so far," Jessie volunteered.

"That is a great start," he commented, looking over the list. "Why don't you take this a step further this week and see if you can determine the factors that impact retention and retrieval? That might be helpful information as well."

"That sounds like an interesting activity," Jessie agreed.

"But what I really wanted to discuss with you this week is what I have been reading," the principal continued. "As you know, we have never had an academic coach at the school before. So I have been doing some reading to try to develop a better understanding of the types of roles the academic coach can play. I would like to give you this book to read. In it there is a chapter that describes the six different types of coaching roles. After you read it, see which role you think would work best here and why. It might end up not being one specific role, but a combination of roles, and that would be fine, too. But I think we should discuss it next week."

"That's a great idea. I think it will really help me to see what the possible roles are so that I know how to more effectively serve our faculty," Jessie agreed. "We looked at these last week during our coaches' meeting, but I would like to spend some additional time thinking about them," she admitted. "I was feeling like I was on information overload by the end of the meeting, so I am sure it would be helpful to have the opportunity to process it more slowly."

Learning Climate

Jessie had begun looking at some of the factors that impact short-term memory. But learning also involves moving information to long-term memory and being able to retrieve it when needed in other situations. The learning environment or climate has a direct impact on the ability to recall information. Not only should the learning environment be positive and supportive, but new information should also be presented in a logistical manner so students can easily place their newly gained knowledge into the correct schemata they use in their long-term memory. Or they may need to construct new general and specific schema for storing this information in their long-term memory. To store information effectively and efficiently, new information must be presented to students in a logical progression.

If information is not presented in this logical, easy-to-be-understood manner, students may become confused and classify the information in incorrect schemata, impeding their knowledge retrieval. For example, if students incorrectly learn that spiders are insects, they will assume that spiders have the same characteristics as insects. Examples of this incorrect classification are evident in errors we hear as students are learning the past tense. You might hear a child say, "I goed down the street." The child has learned how to form the past tense by adding the "ed," but she has not realized that the past tense of "go" is the irregular form "went."

However, learning is more than just a cognitive process. Emotions can affect the learning process as well. "Emotions interact with reason to support or inhibit learning" (Sousa, 2011, p. 48). Creating a positive learning environment results in positive implicit memories associated with the information being presented. Learning should be fun!

Retention

The way in which the learner processes information can have a great impact on the quality of the learning. However, learning and retention are not the same. Retention happens when the learner not only pays attention to the information but also builds the conceptual framework or schemata to consolidate the information in his long-term storage networks. This continued reprocessing of information is referred to as rehearsal, which can be either rote or elaborative.

Rote Rehearsal

Rote rehearsal occurs when the information needs to be stored in specific schema exactly the way it was learned so that it can be used that way in the future. Steps in a procedure or multiplication facts are often learned this way. These rote rehearsals might occur as a result of either simple or cumulative repetitions (Sousa, 2011).

Elaborative Rehearsal

Elaborative rehearsal could include paraphrasing, note taking, predicting, questioning, or summarizing. This type of rehearsal is effective when the information does not necessarily need to be used in the same way as it was learned. Often classroom situations require teachers to adapt the strategies and skills they have learned to meet the needs of different groups of students. During professional development, coaches need to provide opportunities for elaborative rehearsals because instructional strategies require more complex thinking processes where teachers need to be able to apply information from professional development in a new situation. Effective instruction requires more than just applying the steps of a specific procedure. In addition, the information can then be placed in numerous schemata applicable to the specific topic. For example, anticipation guides

CHAPTER FIVE

are a great before-reading strategy. However, they are also great for increasing student engagement, encouraging oral language development, and helping to organize information. So that one strategy might be placed in four different schemas.

Serial Position Effect

The primacy-recency or the serial position effect states that the learner tends to remember most clearly what comes first in an instructional session. Information presented at the end of the session is the next easiest to remember. However, information from the middle of the session is the most difficult to remember (Sousa, 2011).

Researchers investigated the serial position effect and found that there is a higher probability of effective teaching and a shorter portion of downtime when instructional sessions are shorter. For example, learners retain a higher percentage of the information from twenty-minute sessions than they do from forty-minute sessions.

Instructional Methods

However, to be most effective, activities within each of these shorter blocks of instruction should be varied (Sousa, 2011). Coaches might want to vary professional development activities by including such strategies as teacher talk, research, cooperative groups, reading, computer work, journal writing, guest speakers, jigsaw combinations, role-playing, or instructional games.

The learner's ability to retain information is also impacted by the teaching method being used. Lecture or direct instruction seems to result in the lowest levels of information retention. Retention can be supported by rote rehearsal, which occurs during lectures as students are transferring the lecture information into notes; however, in a lecture format there is little opportunity for elaborative rehearsal. The coach's goal in professional development should be to enhance retention.

Multisensory Approaches

There are numerous ways to enhance retention through incorporating additional modalities. Adding visual materials to the presentation tends to increase retention because language and visual information are stored in different areas of the brain. Learning by doing is an effective way to increase sensory input. This approach allows the learner to incorporate kinesthetic and tactile activities, thus including four of the five senses. Structuring instruction to include opportunities for practice and teaching others will also increase retention because it is a more multisensory approach to learning.

Learning and Motor Skills

Learning a motor skill, such as typing or operating a software program, involves following a set of procedures that will eventually be carried out without conscious thought about the steps in the process. Continued practice of the skill changes the brain structurally so that the task can be performed automatically. Through repeated practice, new brain pathways are formed (Sousa, 2011).

If you need to teach two similar skills, it is important to allow time for the learner to master the first skill before the second is introduced. Practice is important, but practice does not always make perfect. If the learner gets confused about the two similar processes, the practice will help to make the mistake permanent. For example, latitude and longitude are typically taught together; consequently, learners tend to easily confuse the two terms.

Hunter (2004) indicated that for practice to improve performance, the learner must want to improve. The learner must understand the ways the information can be applied, how to apply it in a specific situation, and be able to analyze it to determine what needs to be improved. Practices that are close together, or massed practice, help to produce fast learning, while distributed practice over a longer time period helps to increase retention for a longer period of time.

Factors Impacting Retrieval Rates

There needs to be a cue to stimulate the retrieval of information from long-term memory; however, various factors can impact this retrieval rate. People who are in a sad mood more easily remember and focus on negative experiences, while people who are happy tend to remember the

CHAPTER FIVE

pleasant experiences. Similarities between the learning context and the application context tend to increase ease of retrieval. A person's interests and experiences also influence ease of retention. Most important, placing information in the correct schema in the long-term memory provides the highest retrieval rate for the learner. Retrieval is impacted by interests, similar situations, emotional state, and organization. Coaches can enhance retrieval rates by choosing instructional strategies that help learners know how to organize and consolidate the learning.

Our learning and retention is limited by our attention span, our working memory, and our long-term memory. Isolated pieces of information can be difficult to remember. Chunking information enables us to work with larger blocks or amounts of information at one time. We have all been irritated with ourselves for forgetting details. However, forgetting serves an important purpose, too. Forgetting trivial information allows us to focus on the information we view as important (Sousa, 2011).

Structuring Professional Development

An understanding of memory, learning, and retention forms the basis for effective professional development. The professional development content should be structured in the same way as the gradual release process that teachers implement in their classroom when teaching a new strategy or skill. During professional development sessions, coaches need to provide teachers with opportunities to observe the strategies or ideas in action and then practice the strategies in a safe environment.

The first stage would be the I Do step in the gradual release process. However, simply seeing a strategy on a video or seeing it modeled does not provide enough support for teachers to be able to use the strategy independently in their own classroom. Teachers should then be given opportunities to attempt the strategies with peer support during the session and/or in their own classrooms. That would be the We Do step. Finally they will be ready to attempt the new strategy or skill independently, which would be the You Do step of the gradual release process (Pearson & Gallagher, 1983).

Professional development could also be effectively structured to follow Fisher's (2008) four-step gradual release model: I Do, We Do, We

Do Together, and You Do. One of the strengths of Fisher's model is the We Do Together phase, which encourages teachers to collaborate before they attempt the new idea or strategy on their own. In addition, teachers need opportunities to reflect on the content and strategies, their implementation, and their effectiveness in the personal classroom setting.

Using the Gradual Release Model to Plan Professional Development

When planning for professional development, it is important to add a step before and after the gradual release model, whether you are planning a training session, a workshop, or an individual coaching session (Hasbrouck & Denton, 2005). The initial data analysis and purpose-setting phase and the final reflection and evaluation steps would be important to consider in any type of coaching situation, whether it is a workshop, study group, in-class modeling, or co-teaching. Incorporating each step will help teachers be able to apply the ideas independently in their own classrooms.

Establish the Purpose

The step that precedes the gradual release model is examining the data and establishing the purpose for the coaching session (Hasbrouck & Denton, 2005). To increase teacher buy-in, it would be important to discuss the benefits, link the activity to identified needs, focus on student outcomes, and examine the research that supports the activity. Establishing the purpose will make the activity practical for teachers. It is important to illustrate how implementing this strategy, concept, or idea will help teachers to be more successful with their students.

I Do

Once the purpose has been established, the next step in structuring the professional development is the implementation of the gradual release model. The instructional strategies or activities should be modeled for the teachers so that all procedures and steps are clearly presented (Hasbrouck

& Denton, 2005). This modeling can be accomplished through either a live presentation or a video. However, it is even more effective if you can get the teachers' peers and colleagues at their work site to demonstrate their use of the strategy with the specific student population. Because every group of learners is different, teachers need to see how the strategy can work with the students in their subject area and/or classroom to address their specific needs. This would occur during the I Do stage of the gradual release model.

We Do

However, just providing the I Do example is not enough. Professional development needs to be more than just "sit and get." The coach needs to provide opportunities for active involvement where the teachers can practice the strategy in a safe and supportive environment. In addition, the coach should provide opportunities for discussion and involvement with other teachers about the specific strategy. Having teachers sequence the steps in the strategy or role-play its application is one possible way this can occur. In addition, teachers could work together to identify groups of students who would profit from using the strategy and then create lesson plans or activities for those students incorporating the instructional strategy being discussed.

These are great first steps toward developing teachers' confidence in using the new instructional practices being presented. Teachers could then role-play the strategy and discuss ways to apply it in their classroom. This would be the We Do step in the gradual release model, where the teachers are working together with the coach's support. However, merely providing support during the professional development session is not enough, either.

We Do Together

Providing or encouraging additional opportunities to collaborate with other teachers would be a great way to support the We Do Together step in the gradual release model. This could also occur by having the coach co-teach a lesson using the strategy or allowing for peer teachers to work together on the classroom implementation.

You Do

This would lead to the fourth step, You Do, where teachers use the strategy in their own classroom. This would allow them the opportunity to attempt the strategy with their own students.

Reflection

However, there needs to be one final step that follows the gradual release model. During this step, teachers are encouraged to analyze the data and reflect on how effectively the strategy worked during the classroom implementation (Hasbrouck & Denton, 2005). This step can be accomplished through reflecting about either live or taped lessons demonstrating the strategy, as well as by encouraging teachers to reflect on what worked well in their classroom application of the strategy. To encourage teachers to share their thoughts with others, it is important to provide time for individual written reflection before group sharing. Scheduling specific time during the professional development for individual thought tends to increase the likelihood of reflection actually occurring (Spaulding & Smith, 2012). When reflection is planned for outside of the professional development sessions, teachers may become busy and the reflection phase gets overlooked.

Types of Coaching

All coaching is about professional development, but as Kathryn explained to Jessie in the scenario in chapter 4, not all coaching occurs in the same way. Vogt and Shearer (2011) developed a continuum that identified six different types of literacy coaching that could apply to any area of academic coaching. They have arranged these along a continuum from informal to formal coaching.

Informal Coaching Model

Vogt and Shearer's (2011) continuum begins with the *informal coaching model*. In this model, coaching occurs as the coach supports teachers outside of the classroom setting. While conferencing with the teacher, the coach is a co-learner who helps to identify materials and develop curriculum based upon teacher need. The coach assists the teacher in self-assessment and helps the teacher to identify ways to assess students or develop curriculum (Vogt & Shearer, 2011).

Mixed Model of Informal and Formal Coaching

In the *mixed model of informal and formal coaching*, the coach provides support for teachers mainly outside of the classroom, but this is supplemented with some classroom observation. The coach's activities outside of the classroom might include co-planning and leading study groups as a knowledgeable co-learner. As in the last model, most of the coaching activities are occurring outside of the classroom, but the coach may assist within the classroom at the teacher's request (Vogt & Shearer, 2011).

Formal Literacy Coaching Model

The coach, in the *formal literacy coaching model*, primarily supports teachers within the classroom by modeling lessons, conferring with teachers, and coordinating study groups. These activities provide opportunities for focused feedback to assist the teacher in growth in his instructional practice (Vogt & Shearer, 2011).

Peer Coaching and Mentoring Model

The *peer coaching and mentoring model* places the coach in a mentoring role supporting teachers in the classroom. In this model, the coach is viewed as an experienced educator who maintains a nonjudgmental attitude while observing lessons and providing feedback focused on improving instruction. The coach assists teachers in meeting the administrative or school-wide goals (Vogt & Shearer, 2011).

Cognitive Coaching Model

The *cognitive coaching model* views the coach as an observer of the instructor's teaching practice. The coach provides focused feedback to the teacher regarding the best cognitive practices to use in the classroom. As an experienced educator, the coach helps to provide focused teacher feedback in a structured planning, observation, and reflection cycle based on the teacher's perceptions (Vogt & Shearer, 2011).

CHAPTER FIVE

Clinical Supervision Model

The coach, in the *clinical supervision model*, evaluates lessons and provides formal feedback on classroom instruction and teaching practices. At this far end of the continuum, the coach is actually assuming more of an administrative role and less of a coaching role (Vogt & Shearer, 2011).

Although Vogt and Shearer (2011) present six different coaching models, in actual practice a coach might be called upon to fulfill roles or functions from different models, as Jessie's principal observed at the beginning of this chapter. By examining the coach's job description, you will be better able to identify which of the coaching models the school or district is expecting the coach to employ.

Coaching Continuum of Learning Formats

Moran (2007) also developed an eight-part coaching continuum, but her continuum is based on the types of learning formats being implemented by the coach rather than focusing on a description of the coach's role (appendix C). The continuum progresses from collaborative resource manager, to presenter of literacy workshops and professional development sessions, then the continuum moves to focused classroom visits. After the classroom visits, the coach will co-plan with the teachers. As a follow-up activity, coaches could then lead or facilitate study groups to address specific learning concerns. All of the previous portions of the continuum occurred outside of the actual classroom setting.

The coach can then move into the classroom to provide support through demonstration lessons. The demonstration lessons naturally lead into peer coaching, in which the coach observes a lesson, and finally co-teaching, with the coach and the teacher working together to present the lesson. These steps involve a gradual progression in the amount of learning support provided by the coach and how much the coach is involved in the classroom teaching environment (Moran, 2007).

Moran's (2007) continuum is particularly helpful in generating ideas about methods coaches might use for providing teacher support. A coach might not, and probably should not, choose to use the same activities to reach each teacher. The support provided by the coach would differ depending on how receptive the teacher is to the coaching process. Moran's continuum is based on the understanding that a single coaching model will not meet the needs of each teacher. All teachers might not be equally receptive to coaching activities or need the same type of support. Consequently, the coach needs to determine the most effective mode for working with each individual teacher.

The coach's function in Moran's (2007) continuum of coaching is different for each method of teacher interaction and support. When coaches act as collaborative resource managers, for example, they work with teachers to identify available resources that can be used to provide instruction, group learners, and differentiate instruction. When focusing on literacy presentations, they act as facilitators and resource managers who can provide content knowledge while fostering collaboration. The coaches attempt to ensure that all teachers possess the required knowledge so they can implement best practices.

During focused classroom visits, coaches function as both facilitators and resource managers. The coaches provide teachers with opportunities to see various practices being implemented. Usually it is most effective if these can occur in the teachers' classrooms with their students. During the co-planning stage, coaches fill dual roles. They again function as resource managers, but they are also collaborators working with teachers. The coaches and the teachers work together as they review student data and plan for instruction.

When coaches are involved in study groups, they might fill any of three roles: facilitators, mediators, or resource personnel. Together the coaches and teachers meet on a regular basis to discuss issues related to instructional practice. During demonstration lessons, coaches act as expert consultants and presenters. Coaches can demonstrate specific teaching methods for those teachers who might be unfamiliar with them. Coaches act as the experts and as encouragers during peer coaching. The peer-coaching model embodies what has been typically viewed as the coaching model. The coach observes the classroom teacher and then provides feedback. The final format in the continuum in Moran's (2007) model is co-teaching, where coaches act as collaborators and encouragers throughout the planning, implementation, and evaluation of the lesson.

Coaching can occur in many different settings using many different formats. Coaches need to be familiar with each of these possible formats so that they can determine which approach would be most effective in each setting with specific teachers.

Reflect and Apply Activities

5.1. Analyze a professional development you attended or watched online using appendix B. How was information structured to incorporate the concepts of long- and short-term memory? If you don't think these were addressed effectively, how could the professional development have been revised to better address these concepts?

5.2. Read the district job description for an academic or instructional coach. Based on the job description, decide which of Vogt and Shearer's (2011) coaching models it most closely represents and why.

5.3. Interview an instructional coach. Based on the coach's description of the activities from the last week, use the checklist for Moran's (2007) Continuum of Learning Formats (appendix C) by recording a tally mark for each activity described. Then determine the percentage of the frequency for each type of activity.

References

Fisher, D. (2008). *Effective use of the gradual release of responsibility model.* Macmillan/McGraw-Hill Glenco. Retrieved from https://www.mheonline.com/_treasures/pdf/douglas_fisher.pdf.

Hasbrouck, J., & Denton, C. (2005). *The reading coach: A how-to manual for success.* Longmont, CO: Sopris West.

Hunter, M. (2004). *Mastery teaching.* Thousand Oaks, CA: Corwin.

Moran, C. M. (2007). *Differentiated literacy coaching.* Alexandria, VA: Association for Supervision and Curriculum Development. Retrieved from http://www.ascd.org/publications/books/107053/chapters/The-Context-for-a-Literacy-Coaching-Continuum.aspx.

Pearson, P. D., & Gallagher, M. (1983). The instruction of reading comprehension. *Contemporary Educational Psychology, 8,* 317–44.

CHAPTER FIVE

Sousa, D. A. (2011). *How the brain learns* (4th ed.). Thousand Oaks, CA: Corwin.

Spaulding, D. T., & Smith, G. (2012). *Instructional coaches and the instructional leadership team: A guide for school-building improvement.* Thousand Oaks, CA: Corwin.

Vogt, M., & Shearer, B. (2011). *Reading specialists and literacy coaches in the real world* (3rd ed.). Boston, MA: Pearson Education.

CHAPTER SIX

Jessie had spent the past week getting to know most of the staff members, and she felt like she was starting to make some headway with them. Some of them were receptive, others were just polite; however, there were one or two who seemed downright hostile. The coaches' meeting last week had been helpful. Kathryn had talked about the coaching cycle and data analysis. Jessie felt like she had been able to develop a better understanding of both of these processes.

But as she thought about her job, the whole instructional coaching process still seemed a little overwhelming. The staff was composed of ninety-two teachers, and there was only one of her. Jeff Banks had complained that the material he had on photosynthesis for his fourth graders was too difficult for his students, and he had asked whether there were other sources available. She had just spent Jeff's planning period with him discussing some materials that he might find more useful. As she walked down the hall from Jeff's room, Jessie pondered how she was going to support so many teachers and how she should keep track of everything so that nothing fell through the cracks.

"Jessie," the principal stopped her as she passed him. "We have been working in a lot of different areas, but I don't feel we really have a plan for the professional development we are going to provide. We need to develop some specific plans for next steps in that area. How do you think we should proceed? Based on the phone call I just got from district, things don't look good. We really need to see a significant improvement in test scores this year! After four years of our test scores not meeting

CHAPTER SIX

the state standard, if we don't see a change soon, we are going to be looking at a state takeover."

"Have you identified the exact areas where we need to make changes to bring about academic growth?" Jessie asked hopefully, thinking back on what she had just learned about data analysis.

"Well, we have some teachers I am concerned about. You could go in and observe them to see what the problem is," he suggested. "Then you can tell me what you see."

No, she thought. *I certainly will not get very far going into classrooms as his spy.* "Well," she began hesitantly, "if we are being judged on school-wide test scores, it seems like it might be helpful to examine the test data more specifically. Perhaps we could do both a cohort and a longitudinal analysis of the state assessment scores," she suggested, purposely ignoring his last comment. "That would give us information about the specific needs of each grade and how each group of students has performed over time," she continued.

"It doesn't seem like just analyzing the scores is going to get us far. How do we get the teachers to change what they are doing, rather than just giving lip service to the change?" the principal asked in frustration. "You weren't here, so you wouldn't know, but I have hosted a lot of professional development sessions over the last two years. The teachers seem to sit politely through the sessions and then go back to their room and do what they have always done," he added. "Perhaps you could talk about the list of learning characteristics you have been developing."

"How did you determine last year what issues to address during the professional development sessions?" Jessie asked.

"Well, that was easy. We covered all of the topics mandated by the district for that year. If the district said to provide a specific professional development because it was a great strategy, we did!" the principal continued. "I am willing to provide anything my staff needs to be successful!" he added emphatically. "Our students deserve the best education possible."

"Yes, they certainly do," Jessie agreed. "It is really evident that many of the teachers are really concerned about their students. From the conversations I have had, I can tell the teachers seem really focused on student success," she added. "This is just a thought," she continued cautiously, "but have you asked the teachers what they feel they need?"

CHAPTER SIX

"I have talked to many of them. But every time I talk to someone, they tell me something different," he complained. "I can't do everything they suggest. And they never implement any of the new ideas, anyway!"

"This conversation has certainly given me a lot to think about and investigate. How did you determine that the teachers did not implement what was suggested?" Jessie asked, attempting to get some additional information.

"The state assessment data certainly is not improving," the principal complained.

"Over the next few days, let me look at all the data we have available in addition to the state data and see whether that provides any insights," Jessie suggested. As the conversation came to an end and she moved further down the hall, she wondered exactly what data the school had been collecting.

Methods of Data Collection

Coaching typically is provided based upon teachers' felt needs and the school's or the individual student's data. In order to be effective, coaches must understand what data to consider as well as how to analyze and interpret it. In chapter 4, we looked at various ways to disaggregate data: trend, cohort, and longitudinal analysis (Spaulding & Smith, 2012). By disaggregating data, we can analyze the progress of various subgroups whether they are grade levels, students with disabilities, English language learners (ELL), or socioeconomic- or gender-based groups. With the emphasis currently being placed on data-driven instruction, student data from state-administered summative assessments is an effective way of examining student achievement, and it is a great starting point, but it is not the only area to consider.

Formal and Informal Assessments

There are many ways data can be collected using both formal and informal assessments. Formal assessments typically are used as a systematic way to evaluate student performance (Education Place, 1997). These formal assessments follow a prescribed protocol. They could be teacher, school, district, state, or publisher created. Formal assessments are used within the classroom to determine report card grades as well as to rate academic performance.

However, standardized achievement tests and state assessments are also formal assessments. These assessments are typically used by grade or school-wide. Formal standardized assessments are those that have been used with a large sample of students over a period of time so that enough data has been collected for the results to be standardized. Typically the results from standardized formal assessments will be reported in percentiles, stanines, achievement levels, and/or standard scores. The data from these formal assessments provides the information needed to direct instructional decisions. Formal standardized assessments can be used to determine overall achievement or to compare a student's performance to others in his group or in relation to a specific standard.

Norm- and Criterion-Referenced Assessments

Formal assessments encompass both norm- and criterion-reference measures. Results from norm-referenced assessments are used to rank students with respect to achievement. Norm-referenced assessments typically compare a student's performance to that of his age or grade-level peers. These assessments measure a broad range of skills using items that vary in difficulty in an attempt to distinguish between high- and low-performing students. However, data is typically not generated relative to the specific skills needed to master individual standards (Huitt, 1996). Intelligence and developmental screening tests are examples of norm-referenced tests.

Criterion-referenced assessments are used to determine whether specific skills or criteria have been mastered. An individual's performance is compared to the predetermined standard for acceptable performance rather than comparing the student's performance to that of others (Huitt, 1996). Many state assessments are criterion-referenced exams.

Types of Formal Assessments

Formal assessments, whether they are criterion- or norm-referenced, can be used for four different purposes. It is important to choose the assessment that will provide the data at the correct specificity to inform your instruction. These assessments need to be reliable and valid. An assessment is considered reliable if, when the assessment is administered multiple times to the same student, the student earns approximately the same results each time. Assessments are considered valid if they assess what they claim to measure (Pinellas County School District, n.d.).

Screening Assessments

Some assessments are used for screening purposes. These assessments are typically brief and easy to administer. They need to be reliable and able to be repeated. They need to have scores that can be obtained quickly, so that they provide an accurate picture of the student's strengths and weaknesses rather than having to wait months for the arrival of the state summative assessments. These screening assessments are typically administered to all students. Those screening assessments used in the literacy area measure skills such as phonological awareness, letter knowledge, and oral reading fluency because these skills tend to be good predictors of future reading performance. Screening assessments would include such formal assessments as Aimsweb (2014), DIBELS (Good & Kaminski, 2006), and the Gray Oral Reading Test (Wiederholt & Bryant, 2001). Some informal literacy screening assessments such as letter knowledge, sight-word lists, and running records can be used, but the results from these assessments would not be considered as valid since informal assessments have not undergone psychometric analysis to determine validity. The administration procedures on informal assessments are not as formalized; consequently, an informal assessment allows for more possible variation between assessors' scores (SERC, 2012).

Diagnostic Assessments

When difficulties are identified using the results from screening assessments, diagnostic assessment can be used to identify the reasons why students are experiencing difficulty. Diagnostics assessments are given to specific students to determine strengths and areas of need so that appropriate instruction can be provided.

Diagnostic assessments would include such assessments as the Diagnostic Assessment of Reading (DAR, 2006), the Iowa Tests of Basic Skills (2001), the Woodcock Reading Mastery Tests (Woodcock, 2011), and the Words Their Way spelling inventory (Bear & Invernizzi, 2008).

Additional informal literacy measures could include oral reading and use of context clues. However, since these are informal measures, they have not undergone the psychometric analysis to determine validity, reliability, or norming levels (SERC, 2012).

Progress-Monitoring Assessments

Progress-monitoring assessments are used regularly throughout the school year to determine the amount of the student's academic growth since the last testing period. These assessments provide information about the efficacy of the instruction and yield specific information about mastery of individual skills. Progress-monitoring assessments are constructed so that they can be used to generate data that is specific enough to measure small increments of growth. Progress-monitoring assessments would include Aimsweb (2014), running records, and curriculum-based measures (CBM; Intervention Central, n.d.). Informal progress-monitoring tools could include student work samples, interviews, teacher observation, and portfolios (SERC, 2012).

Summative/Evaluative/Outcome Assessments

The final type of assessments can be described using multiple terms. The terms *summative, evaluative,* or *outcome* assessments are used to describe the same type of assessments and the terms are often used interchangeably. A summative assessment is used to determine whether a program or series of instruction has been effective in helping students reach the desired goals. These outcome assessments are typically used at the end of the year or the end of a unit. In addition, at times these summative assessment scores have also been used to determine the next year's placement or to assign a grade to the school.

Types of Informal Assessments

Informal assessments, on the other hand, are more content and performance driven rather than being strictly data driven. A running record, portfolio, interview, group project, survey, or teacher observation would be an example of an informal assessment. The results from these assessments can generate helpful information for guiding instruction (Education Place, 1997). Sometimes informal assessments can be used to generate diagnostic data that has not been captured through other types of assessments.

Levels of Data Analysis

Each state has its own version of accountability data. Some of this accountability data is generated through statewide high-stakes assessments. The data from the state assessments is typically reported at the student, class, school, district, and state levels.

School and District Data

At the school and district levels, data from these state assessments can be used to help identify trends in academic performance. However, typically the state assessment data provides little information about the reasons for the performance data. In addition, there is generally a delay in receiving these results. They often come after the school year is completed, so they are too late to be used to address current academic concerns. In addition to data about school academic performance, school-level accountability data might include attendance records, discipline data, and demographic data such as free/reduced lunch, ethnicity, educational support services, and so on.

Class Data

Data can be analyzed at the classroom level, in addition to the school level. The classroom-level data provides information about the achievement level of individual classes on daily academic activities. These data sources could include class averages, individual chapter tests and quizzes, progress-monitoring results, or state assessments.

Student Data

Student-level data could include such items as individual scores on classroom assessments, attendance, homework completion, or behavioral

CHAPTER SIX

issues. This data can provide information about how an individual student is performing while helping to identify specific barriers to academic success. Student-level data could also include progress monitoring of daily successes and challenges through the use of such methods as reflective journals or scales. These methods are more qualitative and allow the students to examine and reflect on the importance and significance of their academic progress.

Can Instruction Really Make a Difference?

Research has shown that high-quality intensive intervention actually changes the way a student's brain functions. Shaywitz and Shaywitz (2004) in their functional magnetic resonance imaging (fMRI) studies revealed striking differences in the ways that dyslexic and nondyslexic readers processed reading information. During reading the brain activity of the dyslexic and nondyslexic readers differed. Nondyslexic readers experienced activity in the left Broca's area and the left parietotemporal and occipitotemporal areas of their brain, while dyslexic readers display overactivity in the frontal area of the brain. The dyslexic readers demonstrated very little activity in the left-rear areas of the brain that typical readers used. Shaywitz and Shaywitz's (2004) findings suggested that the brains of dyslexic readers attempted to compensate for the lack of use in some areas of the brain by overactivating Broca's area on both sides of the brain.

In their study, Shaywitz and Shaywitz (2004) provided 144 second- and third-grade struggling readers with fifty minutes of daily individual tutoring provided by trained and certified teachers. This tutoring focused on the alphabetic principal and how letters and letter combinations are used to represent the speech sounds. This instruction was provided in addition to the regular classroom reading instruction.

After about eight months, or approximately one hundred hours of instruction, the students in the study demonstrated significant gains in reading fluency. In addition, brain scans showed new activity in the left-rear parietotemporal and occipitotemporal areas that had not been present prior to the tutoring. One year following the study, the students were reading accurately and fluently without any additional tutoring, and fMRI scans revealed that all three left-sided areas of their brains showed brain activity similar to that in normal readers.

The control group that had not received the additional instruction focused on the alphabetic principal and the understanding of letter and letter combinations did not show changes in the fMRI scans of their brain function. The findings of this study demonstrated that appropriate effective reading instruction can have significant impact on brain activity. After receiving small-group intervention, the brains of students with severe reading problems demonstrated reading brain activity that was similar to that of normal readers (Tankersley, 2005). The fMRI scans indicated that appropriate instruction had the power to change the way a person's brain works.

Historically, education has tended to adopt a "wait and see" attitude in attempting to determine whether students will outgrow their reading problems before intervention is provided. We know that all students do not mature at the same rate, so it seemed appropriate to provide additional time before intervention. *Leo the Late Bloomer* (Kraus, 1971) is a cute story, but "waiting for a student to bloom" often does not work. Research indicates that we need to provide assistance as soon as we are aware of the problem. The sooner we provide instruction, the less instruction the students will miss, so the easier it will be to close the gap between where they are and where they need to be. Consequently, it is so important for the coach to be able to understand and analyze all forms of student data. If the specific areas of difficulty can be identified, intervention can be provided before the gap becomes too wide.

Collecting Teacher Data

But student data is not the only school data that needs to be examined. Coaches also need to be able to gather information about teachers' concerns. This information will help the coach to identify the teachers' areas of felt need. Through talking with each teacher individually, the coach could obtain this information. However, that would require a significant investment of time. A more effective way to collect a lot of information quickly would be through a survey. Surveying all of the teachers on your staff would enable you to collect information from each of them. For this type of survey, the teachers at your school would be your sample population. The goal would be to collect information from as many stakeholders as possible. Some members may choose not to respond, while others may intend to but may just forget.

Anonymous or Identified

When a survey is designed, there are many options you will want to consider. One of the first factors to consider is whether the responses should be anonymous. A lack of anonymity may affect the response rates or the validity of the responses you receive. Teachers may not respond honestly if they are concerned about their responses being reported to administration. When constructing the survey, you will need to decide whether you want a one-time snapshot of what is occurring or whether you want to track responses over time. This will determine whether you need to include identifiers on your survey. If you want to track how individual teachers' attitudes have changed over time, you may need to include identifying information. If you only want to analyze changes in the average staff perception, you will not need identifiers.

Response Type

Secondly, you will want to consider whether to use open-ended questions or have the participants choose from the response choices provided. When structuring closed-response choices, these could be structured to allow for only one response or multiple responses. Responses could be dichotomous, where the answer is one of two choices (yes–no, male–female, and such), or the response could be questions with nominal responses that ask for a category response, such as your favorite form of entertainment. Question responses could be ordinal, where the respondent is asked to rank the choices in order of preference. Or the response choices could be at the interval or frequency level. A Likert scale is one of the most common types of frequency scales. It is an ordinal scale that measures the amount of agreement or disagreement with a statement (McLeod, 2008).

Structuring Questions

Then you will need to consider the specific content, wording, format, and order of your questions in the survey. Hence, there are many factors to consider when constructing your survey. The questions, layout, and answer choices are all important factors to consider. You have numerous options to choose from when designing a survey.

When constructing the questions, the developer must determine whether each question is relevant to the topic. You will need to consider whether the question provides additional information or data related to your specific topic. It is important that each question include only one query. Avoid questions that include the word "and." The respondent might agree with one portion of the statement but disagree with the other. For example, if you were to ask whether the respondent likes pizza and soda, the respondent might like one but not the other. You will also want to consider whether the question is too specific or too general and make sure that it is not biased or loaded (Trochim, 2006).

Question Order

Then you will want to consider the sequence of the questions. Do the questions build on each other or does each question provide separate pieces of information? Beginning the survey with simple, engaging, and interesting questions will help to build rapport and motivation. An attempt should be made to avoid putting several difficult questions together. Place demographic information near the end of the survey, unless it is needed for determining eligibility or for routing through particular questions. Be careful not to place closed-ended questions before open-ended questions because the closed-ended questions can impact the responses to the open-ended questions. Asking specific questions before general questions can impact responses to the open-ended questions (Pew Research Center, 2016).

Collecting your staff's opinions may provide information about their desired interest in professional development topics as well as helping to identify the issues or concerns that they are facing. Data collection and analysis is an important component of a coach's job. Data from many different sources provides the basis for the coaching cycle and professional development. This can be formal data from assessments or informal data collected through surveys, conversations, or interviews.

Reflect and Apply Activities

6.1. Analyze your state assessment. Determine whether the assessment is norm- or criterion-referenced. What factors helped you to determine the classification?

6.2. Analyze your school's progress-monitoring process. What assessments are used for progress monitoring? How frequently are progress-monitoring assessments administered? How closely do the progress-monitoring assessments align with the state assessment?

6.3. Construct an online survey using a software program. Use the survey to determine teachers' areas of concern and desire for professional development. Collect and analyze the data to determine school-wide professional development needs.

References

Aimsweb. (2014). NCS Pearson. Retrieved from http://www.aimsweb.com/.

Bear, D. R., & Invernizzi, M. A. (2008). *Words their way*. San Antonio, TX: Pearson. Retrieved from http://readingandwritingproject.com/public/themes/rwproject/resources/assessments/spelling/spelling_elementary.pdf.

Diagnostic Assessment of Reading (DAR). (2006). Rolling Meadows, IL: Riverside Publishing.

Education Place. (1997). *What are the different forms of authentic assessment?* Houghton Mifflin Harcourt. Retrieved from http://www.eduplace.com/rdg/res/litass/forms.html.

Good, R. H., & Kaminski, R. A. (2006). *DIBELS: Dynamic indicators of basic early literacy skills*. Retrieved from https://dibels.org/dibels.html.

Huitt, W. (1996). Measurement and evaluation: Criterion- versus norm-referenced testing. *Educational Psychology Interactive*. Valdosta, GA: Valdosta State University. Retrieved from http://www.edpsycinteractive.org/topics/measeval/crnmref.html.

Intervention Central. (n.d.). Curriculum based measurement warehouse: Reading, math, and other academic assessments. Retrieved from http://www.interventioncentral.org/curriculum-based-measurement-reading-math-assesment-tests.

Iowa Tests of Basic Skills. (2001). Rolling Meadows, IL: Riverside Publishing.

Kraus, R. (1971). *Leo the late bloomer*. New York: Windmill Books.

McLeod, S. (2008). Likert scale. *Simply Psychology*. Retrieved from http://www.simplypsychology.org/likert-scale.html.

Pew Research Center. (2016). *Question order*. Retrieved from http://www.people-press.org/methodology/questionnaire-design/question-order/.

Pinellas County School District. (n.d.). *Classroom assessment*. Retrieved from http://fcit.usf.edu/assessment/basic/basicc.html.

SERC. (2012). *Elementary assessments: Universal screening, diagnostic, and progress monitoring*. State Education Resource Center of Connecticut. Retrieved from http://www.sde.ct.gov/sde/lib/sde/pdf/curriculum/cali/elementary_assessments_4-9-12.pdf.

Shaywitz, S. E., & Shaywitz, B. A. (2004). Reading disability and the brain. *Educational Leadership, 61*(6), 6–11.

Spaulding, D. T., & Smith, G. (2012). *Instructional coaches and the instructional leadership team: A guide for school-building improvement*. Thousand Oaks, CA: Corwin.

Tankersley, K. (2005). *Literacy strategies for grades 4–12*. Alexandria, VA: Association for Supervision and Curriculum Development.

Trochim, W. M. K. (2006). *Research methods knowledge base: Response format*. Retrieved from http://www.socialresearchmethods.net/kb/quesresp.php.

Wiederholt, L., & Bryant, B. R. (2001). *Gray oral reading test* (4th ed.). Quezon City, Philippines: Psychological Resources Center. Retrieved from http://www.psyresources.com/products/language/gort-4.

Woodcock, R. W. (2011). *Woodcock reading mastery tests* (3rd ed.). San Antonio, TX: Pearson.

CHAPTER SEVEN

"So," the principal asked, "the last time we spoke, you were talking about sending out a survey to the staff to get their input. Can you tell me more about what you found out from the survey you sent out last week?'

"OK," Jessie responded. "First, I decided that I would need an anonymous survey if the teachers were going to be willing to share their ideas. That way no one would feel like they were being thrown under the bus. I thought about doing a pencil-and-paper one and having the teachers drop them off with the secretary, but then I decided to send it out electronically to make sure that it was easy to respond to. By using an electronic form, the teachers could respond when they read their e-mail and they did not need to remember to turn in anything else."

"So how many people responded?" the principal asked. "Sometimes surveys don't have a great response rate. I have seen anything from a 2 percent response rate to a 10 percent response rate as good."

"Actually, I had a great response rate! I was really surprised. Almost sixty out of the ninety-two teachers responded. It seems like that high a response rate would tend to indicate that the teachers are really concerned or interested in this topic. They seemed to want their voices heard and were willing to share their ideas. I think this just illustrates how dedicated our staff really is," Jessie added.

"They really do care about their students," the principal agreed. "They want to make a difference."

"Based upon the responses from the survey, I was able to determine what the teachers view as priorities for their professional development.

I analyzed the data from the survey and identified the most frequent responses. This allowed me to identify the three most frequent responses."

"So what did the teachers say?" the principal asked eagerly.

"The most frequent recurring theme was a desire for more information about the Common Core standards and how they impact their instruction. Next, they indicated concerns about how to help students code texts to support their answers. The third most frequent response was a concern about how to determine the appropriate level of difficulty. The teachers seem to be concerned about knowing how to determine the appropriate level of rigor. This concern seems to also be connected to a concern about differentiating appropriately."

"Those are great areas, but how should we address these?"

"I am not exactly sure yet what the best way is. I was thinking about examining concepts related to adult education this week. I have been working with children for years, and that is really easy," Jessie mused, thinking aloud. "But I am not exactly sure right now of the most effective way to do this with adults. I don't think just giving them an article or presenting a PowerPoint during a staff meeting would effectively meet their needs. I do know that I want to incorporate the ideas we have been talking about in reference to how the brain learns. Let me think about this, and I will get back to you shortly with some ideas."

Learning Styles of Children and Adults

Jessie has identified areas of concern and now she is ready to work with the faculty on these, but she needs to decide the most effective way to present this information. To accomplish this she needs to determine whether teaching children happens in the same way as teaching adults. She has already learned a lot about the learning and remembering process in general.

Cognitive processes of children are similar to those of adults; however, adults tend to be more selective about what they "choose" to learn. Children are like sponges and are excited to learn new information. Older teens and adults may choose to learn only what they feel is applicable for their personal growth. Hence, when teaching adults, it is important to help them understand the significance of what you are teaching; otherwise, they may "tune you out," and all of your instructional efforts will be for naught. When teaching adults, coaches can increase buy-in by specifically discussing what is being taught and why this information would be beneficial to them. Once your group of adults embraces your content, they will become more actively involved in the learning process.

There are three distinctive types of learning styles for all learners, both children and adults: (1) visual, (2) kinesthetic, and (3) auditory. Learners tend to use one modality more frequently than another. However, often learners find it helpful to have material presented using more than one modality.

Visual Learners

Visual learners are most successful when they can actually "see" the material that is being presented. Think about math lessons you have experienced. Often the teacher writes the specific steps for solving the math problem on the board. That is one type of visual support. The teacher might also provide visual support through pictures or graphic organizers. These are examples of some ways teachers might present new information to support the visual learners in their class.

Kinesthetic Learners

Kinesthetic learning involves movement, such as writing. Let's use the math lesson as an example. After seeing the steps written on the board, students might write the steps and the completed math problem on a sheet of paper. By having the students copy the math problem from the board, the teacher is addressing the needs of the kinesthetic learners. Another way for the math teacher to support kinesthetic learners would be to provide manipulatives or to have them act out how to solve the problem. Frequently, students are a combination of visual and kinesthetic learners. One learning style may be stronger than the other when learning new information; however, this combination is the typical balance of learning for most learners. These cognitive processes will allow the information to transfer more easily into the student's long-term memory and be available for retrieval when called upon by the learner.

CHAPTER SEVEN

Auditory Learners

Auditory learners are unique in the sense that they typically do not need to write or see what they are learning. They just need to listen to the teacher, a podcast, or classmates discussing the information. This type of learner can visualize the newly gained knowledge and correctly move this information into long-term memory. Retrieval is immediate and easily accessible.

Most learners are a combination of visual and kinesthetic learners, while few are auditory. However, the auditory learner will also retain information presented using either visual or kinesthetic formats. By combining visual and kinesthetic learning styles, educators can help their students more easily process and retain information. Educators often tend to teach using their own learning style strength rather than making sure to address all of the learning styles. Consequently, learners may not understand and retain the content because the information presented did not address their learning style.

Gardner's Intelligences

Howard Gardner, in 1983, wrote *Frames of Mind: Theory of Multiple Intelligences*. He introduced six intelligences or competencies that he believed all humans possess. Today his list has been expanded to include nine intelligences, and more are believed to exist; yet they are hard to quantify through statistical research. He equated these intelligences with numerous personal learning styles. Gardner believed that students learn in ways that are personally distinctive, and the intelligences or competencies relate to a person's unique aptitude and capabilities, which can determine cognitive strengths and weaknesses.

Gardner's nine multiple intelligences are as follows:

1. *Verbal-linguistic intelligence*—highly developed verbal skills and a strong sensitivity to sounds, meanings, and the rhythms of words.

2. *Logical-mathematical intelligence*—the ability to think conceptually and abstractly, demonstrating the capacity to determine logical/numerical patterns.

3. *Spatial-visual intelligence*—the ability to process information through the use of images and pictures. The learner can visualize accurately and abstractly.

4. *Bodily-kinesthetic intelligence*—capacity to control one's body movements and skillfully handle objects.

5. *Musical intelligence*—having the ability to produce and appreciate rhythm, pitch, and timber, oftentimes without formal musical training.

6. *Interpersonal intelligence*—sometimes referred to as emotional intelligence, this would be the ability to read people and respond appropriately to their moods, beliefs, and thinking processes.

7. *Intrapersonal intelligence*—the capacity to be aware of your personal inner feelings, values, beliefs, and thought processes.

8. *Naturalistic intelligence*—the ability to recognize and categorize plants, animals, and other objects in nature.

9. *Existential intelligence*—having the capacity and ability to investigate deep questions about human existence, such as *What is the meaning of life?* (Businessballs.com, 2009).

Why is it important to know these intelligences when presenting new information to children or adults? "Human potential can be tied to one's preferences to learning; thus Gardner's focus on human potential lies in the fact that people have a unique blend of capabilities and intelligences (skills). Gardner asserts that people who have an affinity towards one of these intelligences do so in concert with the other intelligences as 'they develop and solve problems'" (Businessballs.com, 2009, para. 4).

Hence, knowing the various learning styles and Gardner's nine intelligences can be very useful when developing and designing curriculum, planning instruction, selecting course activities, identifying assessment strategies, planning and presenting professional development, and the list goes on and on. Having this information in your teaching toolkit will allow you to address the learning styles or intelligences of most learners.

CHAPTER SEVEN

Adult Learning Theories

Just like there is no one way to reach every student, there is not one specific way to reach all adults. However, three major adult learning theories have been identified: andragogy, self-directed learning, and transformational learning. Malcolm Knowles (1980) was the first to popularize the idea of adult learning. He contrasted adult learning, or andragogy, with pedagogy, the art of teaching children.

Andragogy

His view of andragogy, or adult learning theory, was built on five concepts: (1) As adults mature, they move from dependence to a greater self-directedness in their learning. (2) Adults use their life experiences to aid their learning. (3) The changes they have experienced in life or social roles provide the basis for new learning. (4) Adults look for immediate application for what they are learning. They are interested in learning things that can be immediately applied to their current position in life. (5) Adults are motivated by internal rather than external factors (Knowles, 1980).

These concepts about andragogy provide the basis for the six recommendations Knowles et al. (1984) made for working with adult learners: (1) Adults learn most effectively when a cooperative climate is encouraged. (2) The learner's specific needs and interests should be addressed. (3) Objectives should be reached through sequential activities that build logically to the final goal. (4) Learners should work collaboratively with the instructor to select methods, materials, and resources. (5) Adult learners appreciate having input into their learning. (6) Finally, the quality of the learning experiences should be evaluated and revised as needed. Adult learners want to know the reason why they are learning something. It is helpful to involve learners in solving real-life problems (American Institutes for Research, 2011).

Self-Directed Learning

Self-directed learning, the second adult learning theory, is a process that typically occurs outside of the traditional classroom setting. In self-directed learning, individual learners determine the content, methods, materials, and evaluation of the learning. This is similar to some of the andragogy ideas presented by Knowles (1980). Self-directed learning can be used to augment or replace traditional learning experiences. During the self-directed process the teacher works with the learner to help to identify objectives, and the starting point; match resources and content; establish learning goals, objectives, and evaluation; develop positive attitudes toward self-direction and independence; and reflect on the instruction (Knowles, 1975).

Transformative Learning

Transformative learning, the third adult learning theory, aims to change the way individuals think about themselves and the world. Freire (2000) viewed transformative learning as freeing because it encouraged learners to strive for social change. Mezirow (2000) discussed responsibilities of learners and facilitators in transformative learning. He encouraged learners to engage in discussions that challenged assumptions and considered various perspectives. He indicated that to foster transformative learning, facilitators needed to create a trusting, caring climate while providing immediate feedback. He stressed that for transformative learning to occur, it is important that the learners feel comfortable having their statements challenged and that opportunities for reflection are included.

Professional Development

Literacy Coach Clearinghouse (2009) identified many areas about adult learning that coaches should understand. The coach's goal is to provide quality professional development with the ultimate goal of increasing student learning. This goal requires an understanding of the components of effective professional development that lead to improved instructional practices implemented by reflective practitioners.

Professional development should focus on supporting the adult learners through respect, confidentiality, planning, stress management, and other incentives. Coaches attempt to use teachers' strengths to bring about change. This may involve managing difficult conversations and attempting to arrive at win-win resolutions in areas of conflict (Literacy Coach Clearinghouse, 2009). This professional development will need to occur in many varied group and presentation formats, whether they be whole group, department/grade-level groups, small groups, or individual sessions. In each learning format, the coach should be gathering, collecting, and analyzing information about the targeted instructional practices through both formal and informal methods.

Coaching Practices

All coaching does not look the same, as we discovered when we examined Moran's (2007) continuum; consequently, coaches need to be able to interact effectively in a variety of settings. Sometimes coaching occurs outside of the classroom through collaborative identification of goals and planning for lessons, assessments, and units. During this process the coach might be involved with an individual teacher or with a team of teachers. Coaches might also be asked to help clarify or mediate the roles and relationships between teachers and administrators. Both teachers and administrators have the students' best interest in mind, but because of differences in perspectives, both parties might not see issues from the same vantage point. Since the coach is a teacher who works closely with administration, she often ends up hearing both teacher and administrative perspectives and can verbalize the concerns of each group.

As we have observed, the coach can be asked to fill many different coaching roles. However, in each of the different coaching methods, the coach needs to be proficient with observational practices. An understanding of observation protocols and reflective dialogues is imperative since coaches spend much of their time observing. Sometimes simply observing a lesson is not enough support; however, this observational process helps the coach determine in what area the instructional practices could be refined.

Observational Categories

The coach's observations can be broken down into three major categories. The first would be observations about organizational delivery and timing. This area would include observations about the pacing, scheduling, materials, transitions, grouping, room arrangement, time on task, and so on. The second category would be observations related to the specific content and methods appropriate for that content delivery. The rationale for the delivery and organization of the instructional practices would be the third category. Learning theory related to developing independence leading to flexibility and application in varied settings would be portions of this third category (Puig & Froelich, 2007).

Using Data from Observations

Based on these observations, the coach and the teacher can decide on the next steps in the professional development process. After observing a lesson, the implementation of the gradual release process may begin. The coach could decide, for example, to model a particular strategy in the teacher's classroom so that the teacher develops a better understanding of how to implement a strategy or content knowledge with his specific group of students. The coach might find it helpful to co-teach with the teacher to further scaffold the process. As is true when using the gradual release process with students, each step in this process helps to build the teacher's confidence in the strategy implementation. During the entire process, the coach needs to be able to provide additional coaching on the spot to support the instructional process at the time when the teacher needs it.

Classroom observation might make behavioral concerns evident. Because of their impact on student achievement, discipline or behavioral concerns are another area coaches are often asked to address. Behavioral concerns can be a particularly challenging area for new or beginning teachers; consequently, the coach needs to have a thorough understanding of how to effectively establish classroom routines and policies.

Coaches might also work with teachers to help identify effective methods for data collection before, during, and after instruction. Before the lesson, decisions about content are made based upon data that has been previously collected. During the instructional process, coaches might observe the lesson and be involved in the formative and summative data collection. Finally, after instruction, coaches might facilitate the analysis of the data to determine next steps in instruction (Literacy Coach Clearinghouse, 2009).

The broad objective of coaching is to help teachers to refine their instruction. The National Board of Professional Teaching Standards (2014) has developed five propositions that encompass the qualities that coaches help teachers to develop. These propositions include the following components:

1. Teachers know the subject they teach and have the necessary pedagogical knowledge.
2. Teachers are responsible for managing and monitoring student learning.
3. Teachers are committed to their students and their learning.
4. Teachers think systematically about their practice and learn from experience.
5. Teachers are members of learning communities (para. 4).

These propositions, first published in 1989, provide the basis for the National Board Standards and appear to identify similar components as many of our current teacher evaluation systems.

Teacher Evaluation Systems

In the current standards-based teacher accountability environment, coaching support has become even more important because it provides a method for teachers to refine and improve their instruction. For years teacher evaluation was perfunctory. If a teacher had tenure, the evaluation (assuming it occurred) typically meant little. Funds made available through federal programs such as Race to the Top Fund (US Department of Education, 2010), No Child Left Behind (US Department of Education, 2001), and the Teacher Incentive Fund (US Department of Education, 2014) have resulted in significant changes in teacher evaluation systems. Consequently, in many states teacher performance is now judged based upon student learning outcomes, classroom observations, and other measures (Bornfreund, 2013). These revisions have resulted in changes in the way students' scores on state standardized tests are used, as well as changes in the actual teacher evaluation systems. Coaching in lesson organization, delivery, and learning theory can help to prepare teachers for the teacher evaluation system being used in their state or district.

CHAPTER SEVEN

Individual states have developed various methods for incorporating teacher evaluations and students' state assessment scores into their systems. However, some trends do exist. In their teacher evaluation systems, forty-six of the states include information about teachers' impact on student learning. Thirty-three states require or recommend that teachers be observed at least once a year with many of these states using this information as a basis for evaluating teacher performance and to inform personnel decisions such as license renewal, promotion, teacher assignments, and recognition of highly effective teachers. Thirty-one states use the evaluation result to determine individual teacher's professional development, while in thirty-two states teachers can be terminated as a result of poor evaluations (Hull, 2013).

In addition to state-specific evaluation systems, the literature frequently refers to four teacher evaluation frameworks: Danielson, Marshall, Marzano, and McRel. These systems have been adopted in part or whole in multiple states (National Education Association, 2011). Danielson's framework was developed in 1995 and involves observation of classroom practice supported by discussions between the evaluator and the teachers. Adopted in more than twenty states (Pritchett, 2013), the Danielson framework is aligned with the Interstate Teacher Assessment and Support Consortium (InTASC) standards and is founded on a constructivist view of learning. Its twenty-two components and seventy-six smaller elements are arranged into four domains (Danielson Group, 2013).

Marshall's (2011) framework expands on Danielson's four domains and includes supervision and evaluation with an emphasis on student performance. Rather than focusing on individual classroom observation as Danielson does, the evaluation rubric is used as an end-of-the-year assessment based upon frequent classroom observations by administration. Teachers are evaluated on the ten criteria in each of six domains. The scores from the criteria in each domain are averaged to determine a score for that domain. The criteria scores are used to determine strengths and areas for professional development (Marshall, 2011).

Marzano's teacher evaluation (2013) system collects data through walkthroughs and informal and formal observations. It has been used in numerous schools, districts, and states; in addition, New York, New Jersey, and Florida have adopted parts or the whole of the model on a wider basis. Marzano's model has sixty elements divided between four domains, with forty-one of these being in Domain 1: Classroom Strategies and Behaviors (Marzano, 2013).

The fourth framework, the McRel evaluation system (2012), was developed in North Carolina and promotes effective leadership, quality teaching, and student learning. The twenty-five points from the evaluation system divide the observable teacher practices into five standards, each of which are supported by additional elements. There is a sixth standard that is not included in the teacher evaluation rubric but instead focuses on acceptable, measurable student progress (McRel, 2012).

Although each of the frameworks has its own evaluation and observation system, many of the four have similar components. Table 7.1 compares the four frameworks. Although the number and order of components differ, you will see frequent overlaps in the content. Recurring themes are arranged horizontally across the chart.

Each of the domains or standards has elements and indicators that are used to more specifically develop and explain the components. No matter which teacher evaluation system is used, coaches need to be familiar with the important components so that they can discuss these with teachers. Within the chapters that follow, we will look more specifically at the various components of the four systems.

Reflect and Apply Activities

7.1. Analyze a professional development you attended or watched online. How was information structured to incorporate the different learning styles? If you don't think these were addressed effectively, how could the professional development have been revised to better address these concepts?

7.2. Work with a classroom teacher to create a multiple intelligence unit of work matrix containing activities that students could use to demonstrate content knowledge using multiple intelligences during an instructional unit.

7.3. Analyze the characteristics of the teacher evaluation system used in your state or district. Compare yours to the ones described in this chapter. How can the coach effectively

Table 7.1. Teacher Evaluation Framework by Model

Framework	Danielson Framework for Teaching (Danielson Group, 2013)	Marshall's Framework (Marshall, 2011)	Marzano's Teacher Evaluation System (Marzano, 2013)	McRel Evaluation System (McRel, 2012)
Planning	Domain 1: Planning and Preparation	Domain A: Planning and Preparation for Learning	Domain 2: Planning and Preparing	Standard 4: Teachers facilitate learning for their students
Classroom	Domain 2: Classroom Environment	Domain B: Classroom Management	Domain 1: Classroom Strategies and Behaviors	Standard 2: Teachers establish a respectful environment for a diverse population
Instruction	Domain 3: Instruction	Domain C: Delivery of Instruction	Domain 1: Classroom Strategies and Behaviors	Standard 3: Teachers know the content they teach
Activities Outside the Classroom	Domain 4: Professional Responsibilities	Domain F: Professional Responsibilities	Domain 4: Collegiality and Professionalism	Standard 1: Teachers demonstrate leadership
Assessment and/ or Reflection		Domain D: Monitoring, Assessment, and Follow-up	Domain 3: Reflecting on Teaching	Standard 5: Teachers reflect on their practice
Additional Components		Domain E: Family and Community Outreach		Standard 6: Teachers contribute to the academic success of students

support teachers in the specific evaluation system your school is using?

References

American Institutes for Research. (2011). TEAL Center fact sheet # 11: Adult learning theories. *Teaching Excellence in Adult Literacy.* Retrieved from https://teal.ed.gov/sites/default/files/Fact-Sheets/11_%20TEAL_Adult_Learning_Theory.pdf.

Bornfreund, L. A. (2013). *An ocean of unknowns: Risks and opportunities in using student achievement data to evaluate PreK–3rd grade teachers.* Foundation for Child Development. Retrieved from http://fcd-us.org/sites/default/files/Ocean%20of%20Unknowns-%20Bornfreund.pdf.

Businessballs.com. (2009). *Howard Gardner multiple intelligences.* Retrieved from www.businessballs.com/howardgardnermultipleintelligences.htm.

Danielson Group. (2013). *The framework.* DanielsonGroup.org. Retrieved from https://danielsongroup.org/framework/.

Freire, P. (2000). *Pedagogy of the oppressed. Rev. 30th anniversary ed.* New York: Continuum.

Gardner, H. (1983). *Frames of mind: Theory of multiple intelligences.* New York: Basic Books.

Hull, J. (2013). *Trends in teacher education.* Center for Public Education. Retrieved from http://www.centerforpubliceducation.org/Main-Menu/Evaluating-performance/Trends-in-Teacher-Evaluation-At-A-Glance/Trends-in-Teacher-Evaluation-Full-Report-PDF.pdf.

Knowles, M. (1975). *Self-directed learning: A guide for learners and teachers.* Chicago: Follett.

Knowles, M. (1980). *The modern practice of adult education: Andragogy versus pedagogy. Rev. and updated ed.* Englewood Cliffs, NJ: Cambridge Adult Education.

Knowles, M., et al. (1984). *Andragogy in action: Applying modern principles of adult learning.* San Francisco: Jossey-Bass.

Literacy Coach Clearinghouse. (2009). *Self-assessment for elementary literacy coaches.* Retrieved from http://www.literacycoachingonline.org/briefs/tools/self_assessment_for_elem_lit_coaches.pdf.

Marshall, K. (2011). *Teacher evaluation rubrics.* Retrieved from http://usny.nysed.gov/rttt/teachers-leaders/practicerubrics/Docs/MarshallTeacherRubric.pdf.

Marzano, R. J. (2013). *The Marzano teacher evaluation model*. MarzanoResearch.com. Retrieved from http://tpep-wa.org/wp-content/uploads/Marzano_Teacher_Evaluation_Model.pdf.

McRel. (2012). *North Carolina teacher evaluation process*. Retrieved from http://www.uncfsu.edu/Documents/soe/assessment/teach-eval-manual.pdf.

Mezirow, J. (2000). Learning to think like an adult: Core concepts of transformation theory. In J. Mezirow (Ed.), *Learning as transformation: Critical perspectives on a theory in progress*. San Francisco: Jossey-Bass.

Moran, C. M. (2007). *Differentiated literacy coaching*. Alexandria, VA: Association for Supervision and Curriculum Development. Retrieved from http://www.ascd.org/publications/books/107053/chapters/The-Context-for-a-Literacy-Coaching-Continuum.aspx.

National Board of Professional Teaching Standards. (2014). *Five core propositions*. Retrieved from http://www.nbpts.org/five-core-propositions.

National Education Association. (2011). *Promoting and implementing the National Education Association policy statement of teach evaluation and accountability: An NEA toolkit*. Retrieved from http://www.nea.org/assets/docs/2011NEA_Teacher_Eval_Toolkit.pdf.

Pritchett, B. (2013). *States implement new teacher evaluations that include student performance*. Heartland Institute. Retrieved from https://www.heartland.org/news-opinion/news/states-implement-new-teacher-evaluations-that-include-student-performance.

Puig, E. A., & Froelich, K. S. (2007). *The literacy coach: Guiding in the right direction*. Boston, MA: Pearson Education.

US Department of Education. (2001). *No Child Left Behind Act of 2001*. Retrieved from http://www2.ed.gov/policy/elsec/leg/esea02/index.html.

US Department of Education. (2010). *Race to the Top Fund*. Retrieved from http://www2.ed.gov/programs/racetothetop/index.html.

US Department of Education. (2014). *Teacher Incentive Fund*. Retrieved from http://www2.ed.gov/programs/teacherincentive/index.html.

CHAPTER EIGHT

Jessie rushed into her office, shrugging off her jacket and throwing it over the back of her chair. She had ten minutes before her appointment with Andrea. Jessie was excited about this since Andrea was the first teacher to reach out to her as the coach. Andrea was coming as soon as she dropped her students at PE, so Jessie wanted to make sure she was prepared. She slid into her desk chair and opened her computer to the file that contained the data from Andrea's third-grade class, scanning the list to see how they had done on the progress-monitoring assessment two weeks ago.

Andrea was a first-year teacher, and she had indicated that she was feeling a little overwhelmed and concerned about her students' progress. "Hi, Jessie," Andrea greeted, sticking her head into Jessie's room. "Well, got the class to PE. Now I have forty minutes before they will be back. I guess we need to talk fast. I heard that this is your first year, too, so how's it going for you?" Andrea asked, sliding into an empty seat at the round table.

"Things are going well. I am loving my new job! This is a great school. I have met so many nice staff members," Jessie continued with a smile, joining her at the table. "How are you adjusting?"

"I am excited to have my own classroom. But being a teacher has certainly been a lot harder than I thought it would be. It seemed so easy when I was student teaching. I know the standards I am supposed to be teaching; however, I feel like I am not getting the ideas across to them as clearly as I would like. The students just don't seem to be remembering

CHAPTER EIGHT

the information. I remember my teachers in elementary school gave us a lot of information to remember and we did fine, but my students just can't seem to remember information from one day to the next."

"It sounds like you have been doing a lot of thinking about your instruction. How did your students do on the progress-monitoring assessment last week?" Jessie queried.

"Not really as well as I was hoping," Andrea complained. "But I am not sure what else I can do."

"So what standards or areas do they demonstrate proficiency on? And do you have data from other assessments?" Jessie asked.

"Well, I have been really busy, and there just seems to be too much data to keep straight. I did just finish doing IRIs on a couple of my kiddos that I was really concerned about," she added by way of explanation.

"That was a great idea. I can see you know how to get additional information on these students and are really trying to use the data to drive your instruction. But you're right; the amount of assessment and data can be overwhelming at times."

"Have you decided how to organize the data?"

"Well, I have put the handouts I got with my class's scores from each of the assessments in a folder," Andrea commented, seeming a little confused.

"Sometimes it helps to look at all the data on each student at one time," Jessie suggested. "I have a tool that I use that might make all of this data a little easier to process. We don't have time during this meeting, but would you like to get together to go over this later?"

Components of a Well-Designed Coaching System

We don't really have any information about Andrea's content knowledge, but we do know that she is concerned about her content delivery. Teacher concerns about content delivery and student achievement are probably one of the most common issues coaches are asked to address. In the last chapter, we examined four different teacher evaluation models. We don't know which framework Jessie's school is using, but in order for Jessie to support content delivery, she needs to develop a coaching system based on an understanding of the components of instructional delivery.

CHAPTER EIGHT

The Annenberg Institute for School Reform (n.d.) has identified three components of a well-designed coaching system. These include a "content-based focus on adult learning," "conditions that support effective coaching," and "instructional leadership provided by the coach" (p. 3). To address Andrea's concerns we need to begin by looking at the first component of the coaching system, a content-based focus. This content focus is evident in all four of the teacher evaluation systems. Two of the frameworks address content knowledge specifically, while all four of them focus on the teacher's delivery of that content knowledge.

Content-Based Focus on Adult Learning

McRel (2012) dedicated an entire standard, Standard 3, to teachers' content knowledge. In Standard 3: Teachers Know the Content They Teach, McRel identified four content knowledge-related components. These four components specify that effective teachers need to be able to align their instruction with the standards, they need to know the content, they understand the interconnectedness of the content, and they can make the content relevant to their students (p. 25–26).

Danielson (2013), on the other hand, classified content knowledge as a foundational skill. Danielson's first component of Domain 1: Planning and Preparation is titled Demonstrating Knowledge of Content and Pedagogy (p. 7). In Danielson's model, content knowledge provides the foundation for teacher effectiveness. In addition, Domain 3: Instruction of Danielson's model, similar to Marshall's framework, builds on this content knowledge by examining the teacher's ability to deliver the content through effective communication with students, questioning and discussion, engaging students in learning, using assessment, and demonstrating flexibility and responsiveness (p. 55–79).

Marshall's framework (2011) examined teacher's knowledge based on the teacher's ability to express that content knowledge. Marshall's Delivery of Instruction domain encompasses ten components. These include setting high expectations for all students, developing a growth mindset, identifying the goal of the instruction, building on student interest and connecting to prior knowledge, presenting information clearly, using effective strategies, engaging all students, differentiating, using teachable moments, and involving students in summarizing and internalizing (p. 4).

CHAPTER EIGHT

A portion of Domain 1 in Marzano's (2013) evaluation framework, elements 16–23, focuses on content delivery; however, the teacher's content knowledge is not specifically addressed. Three design questions embody the ideas of elements 16–23: What will I do to help students effectively interact with new knowledge? What will I do to help students practice and deepen their understanding of new knowledge? And what will I do to help students generate and test hypotheses about new knowledge (p. 1)?

The Annenberg Institute for School Reform (n.d.) stressed the importance of providing a "content-based focus on adult learning" (p. 3) to help teachers develop content knowledge supported by data to inform learning and professional development. The institute recommended that coaches use school data to determine the most important strategies to model in classrooms, develop content leadership, and connect content to larger ideas between and among domains. This process should be informed by continued measurement, documentation, and reflection on teacher and student learning.

As we saw in Jessie's conversation with Andrea, data provides the basis for the coaching discussion by focusing on strategic areas of need. This shifts the focus of professional development from teacher deficits to student learning.

Conditions That Support Effective Coaching

For the coaching process to be effective, systems must be in place to support it. These supports should be provided by the district or school initiatives and goals. The coaching process should focus on content and student learning. This allows the impact of coaching to be measured in a slightly more quantifiable way. Data on student achievement helps to make the value of coaching evident to all stakeholders. As we have discussed, since coaches work with adults, coaching needs to support the principles of adult learning. However, an important overlooked component of effective coaching is that coaching and professional development need to occur during dedicated time for groups of teachers to meet and learn together (Annenberg, n.d.). If time is not provided within the school day, it is difficult for teachers to be open to coaching because of other demands on their time.

CHAPTER EIGHT

Instructional Leadership Provided by the Coach

Effective coaching systems must also include "instructional leadership provided by the coach" (Annenberg, n.d., p. 3). Coaches need to have the time to be able to observe instruction and provide feedback to teachers. During this process, coaches should encourage peer observations, provide opportunities for group discussion of the instructional processes, model instructional strategies, and gather data through multiple sources. In addition, to be effective, coaches need time to engage in their own professional development.

To accomplish all of these effectively, coaches must be knowledgeable about content, district reforms, curricular standards, and adult learning. Strong communication and interpersonal skills, ability to analyze data, follow through, and a willingness to learn and listen are all important components coaches need for providing professional leadership (Poglinco et al., 2003).

Teachers at Different Career Stages

Jessie was excited that Andrea came to her looking for help; however, not all teachers are as willing to work with the instructional coach as Andrea was. As you begin working with teachers, you will deal with many different types of teachers. Each teacher is different, but they generally can be divided into the four groups we discussed in chapter 3: eager and open, eager but resistant, reluctant but not resistant, or reluctant and resistant (Hasbrouck & Denton, 2005, p. 25–26).

Andrea would exemplify the eager and open group of teachers. Typically these are beginning teachers who are seeking guidance in developing their craft. Teachers who are in the eager but resistant group realize they are experiencing a problem in their classroom but do not view this problem as something that is impacted by their actions. They view these problems as caused by issues outside of their instructional practice, such as problem students, difficult parents, other teachers, lack of materials, and so forth. These would all be issues outside of their control, so although they want solutions, they are not open to suggestions the coach might have that would require any change on their part.

Reluctant but not resistant teachers would be those teachers who are generally successful in their practice and so don't see a need for the coach's services. Typically they are experienced teachers who have gotten along fine without the coach for quite a few years.

The teacher in the scenario in chapter 1 would exemplify the typical teacher in the reluctant and resistant group. Theses teachers don't want to try out any new ideas and they typically are not open to having another adult in "their" classroom.

Working with Teachers

While in an ideal world, all teachers are eager and open, in reality, not all teachers are. Some simple suggestions may make working with teachers in their classroom easier for the coach. Keep your first visits into the classroom short, simple, and to the point. When you go into a classroom, focus on just one idea. This could be sharing an instructional strategy, but it could also be as simple as recognizing something the teacher does well or just delivering materials the teacher has requested. Do the one thing you came into the room to do and then leave. It is important to respect the teacher's time!

Work on getting to know each staff member. Begin with short "getting to know you" conversations. Strike up brief conversations in the hall or other common areas. It is important to keep the conversation positive. Ask the teacher to share what is going well. Use these short visits as opportunities to build a relationship and to identify teachers' strengths.

Remember that the coach does not have to be the only expert. Sometimes you will want to bring teachers together to share their knowledge. Many times a teacher will be more receptive to ideas that are shared by teachers who teach the same content or grade level. From the coach's perspective, facilitating this peer-coaching process might involve providing coverage so that two teachers can work together.

A teacher's time is precious. Even if you are expected in the room, make sure to remind the teacher why you are there and how long you will be staying. The teacher is busy in her room and could have forgotten what was planned, and this simple step can assure the teacher you will not overstay your welcome.

Coaches need to help teachers be "committed to their students and their learning" and "think systematically about their practice and learn from experience" (National Board of Professional Teaching Standards,

2014). Each of the teacher evaluation frameworks addresses this issue. Danielson's Domain 3 is the Instructional domain and includes communicating clearly, using questioning and discussion strategies, engaging students in learning, providing feedback, and being flexible and responsive to students. So how can coaches help teachers to be committed to their students and their learning? Communicating with learners is an important component of this skill—whether the learners are students or teachers.

Feedback

All communication between coaches, teachers, and students will need to involve feedback in some form. There are three basic types of feedback coaches can provide: "specific praise, instructional scaffolding, and corrective feedback" (Hasbrouck & Denton, 2005, p. 10).

Specific Praise

At the beginning of this chapter Jessie had just started giving Andrea some feedback. Andrea had been concerned about next steps in the instructional process, and Jessie chose to provide specific praise by acknowledging Andrea's attempt to collect additional data. When providing praise, it should be specific and authentic. Andrea had known that she needed more information and had developed a plan for obtaining it. Jessie used specific praise when she acknowledged the important steps Andrea had taken.

Instructional Scaffolding

Jessie expanded on the specific praise by also providing instructional scaffolding. Scaffolding is temporary support that is provided until the individuals are ready to attempt the activity by themselves. Jessie used this when she identified a data organization tool and then offered to teach Andrea how to use it. Jessie scaffolded for success by choosing a tool that she felt Andrea could use effectively. Andrea appears to have concerns about her students' reading performance since she discussed completing informal reading inventories (IRI). Consequently, Jessie made plans to work with Andrea using the tool to collect, organize, and analyze the data. Jessie could choose to use the tools in appendix D or E, depending on

CHAPTER EIGHT

whether Andrea was collecting data using diagnostic tools that contained information about the reading strands or whether her assessments provided data on the literacy standards. Using the templates found in the appendixes will enable Andrea to analyze the performance of the entire class of students to determine which content information needs to be presented whole group and which should be presented in small groups or individually. If Andrea had concerns about mathematics skills, she could use the templates in appendix F or G, depending on which level she was teaching.

After analyzing the data, Andrea can pinpoint specific areas of concern; then Jessie's next step would be to identify strategies to address those specific areas of concern. Jessie would need to scaffold by breaking the strategy into small steps so that it was easy for Andrea to remember the steps of the strategy. During the guided practice part of the gradual release cycle, while Andrea is attempting to use the strategy, Jessie might scaffold by prompting, supplying partial information, or linking the information to something Andrea already knows (Hasbrouck & Denton, 2005). As Jessie develops a plan for working with Andrea, we can see scaffolding occurring in many different ways.

Corrective Feedback

Feedback or scaffolding could also be corrective. Jessie has not used this type of scaffolding with Andrea. This type of feedback could be particularly useful in the coaching process when the teacher does not understand how to effectively present the information or concepts. When we practice a mistake, we tend to make it permanent, and the repeated practice of the mistake makes the process more difficult to correct.

However, choosing the correct amount of wait time before providing correction can be difficult. It is important for the coach not to provide correction too quickly but to allow the teacher time to discover his own errors and learn from them. If the teacher does not see how the instruction can be further refined, then corrective feedback should be provided in a neutral tone so the learner is not discouraged (Hasbrouck & Denton, 2005).

Coaches who want to be effective work to incorporate characteristics that have been found to be important. They provide scaffolding to help teachers analyze and improve their instructional practice and identify tools and strategies to help teachers monitor and improve students' learning.

This professional development could happen on a one-to-one basis, as it did with Andrea, or in a small- or large-group setting. However, one-on-one professional development is probably the easiest way for the coach to begin working with teachers.

Reflect and Apply Activities

8.1. Coaches need content knowledge. Examine the standards for a content area you as the coach would be most likely to observe. Determine how each of these standards is assessed on your state assessment.

8.2. Construct a list of a few people on your staff who you don't know well. Decide how you would structure a "getting to know you" conversation. What would you ask and when and how would you do this? Try this with a couple of the people on your list and reflect on what went well or what could be improved.

8.3. Analyze a lesson you observed in person or watched online. Identify the type of feedback provided: specific praise, instructional scaffolding, or corrective feedback. Which type did the teacher use most frequently? Construct some feedback statements the teacher could have used to provide other types of feedback when working with the students.

References

Annenberg Institute for School Reform. (n.d.). *Instructional coaching: Professional development strategies that improve instruction*. Retrieved from http://annenberginstitute.org/sites/default/files/product/270/files/Instructional Coaching.pdf.
Danielson Group. (2013). *The framework*. DanielsonGroup.org. Retrieved from https://danielsongroup.org/framework/.
Hasbrouck, J., & Denton, C. (2005). *The reading coach: A how-to manual for success*. Longmont, CO: Sopris West.
Marshall, K. (2011). *Teacher evaluation rubrics*. Retrieved from http://usny.nysed.gov/rttt/teachers-leaders/practicerubrics/Docs/MarshallTeacherRubric.pdf.

CHAPTER EIGHT

Marzano, R. J. (2013). *The Marzano teacher evaluation model.* MarzanoResearch.com. Retrieved from http://tpep-wa.org/wp-content/uploads/Marzano_Teacher_Evaluation_Model.pdf.

McRel. (2012). *North Carolina teacher evaluation process.* Retrieved from http://www.uncfsu.edu/Documents/soe/assessment/teach-eval-manual.pdf.

National Board of Professional Teaching Standards. (2014). *Five core propositions.* Retrieved from http://www.nbpts.org/five-core-propositions.

Poglinco, S., Bach, A., Hovde, K., Rosenblum, S., Saunders, M., & Supovitz, J. (2003). *The heart of the matter: The coaching model in America's choice schools.* Philadelphia: Consortium for Policy Research in Education, University of Pennsylvania. Retrieved from www.cpre.org/Publications/Publications_Research.htm.

CHAPTER NINE

Jessie walked into the faculty lounge with her lunch and sat down at a table where Andrea and Thomas were deep in discussion.

"But they just don't seem to remember anything," Andrea continued. "I remember when we were in elementary school we learned the Gettysburg Address, twenty-five new vocabulary words each week, and I don't know what else."

"Well, things have changed since we were kids," Thomas agreed. "Think about when we were growing up. We played outside with the kids in the neighborhood after school, and then we would have dinner together as a family in the evening. Then, as a family, we might watch a television show or read. I don't think many of our students today live in that type of an environment."

"You can say that again," Andrea agreed. "Most of my students don't talk about family dinners or watching TV together. But what does that have to do with learning at school?"

"Probably nothing. I don't know—I am just amazed at the differences. Kids just don't seem to have developed conversational or social skills to the level that would seem appropriate. Most of the kids in my second-grade class have televisions, computers, cell phones, movies, video games, and other technology at their fingertips throughout the day. No longer is technology limited to a short period of time. It seems to influence every waking moment. Children are spending more time indoors with technology and less time developing those gross motor and socializations skills," Thomas lamented.

"Maybe we are not so different," Jessica mused, looking at the TV that was on in the lounge. "Just watching the news is a multifaceted event," she commented. "Just look at that TV screen. It is switching between three or four different reporters commenting from different areas of the world while unrelated news captions are scrolling across the bottom of the screen. At the same time I can get the weather and the stock prices."

The conversation was interrupted as Thomas glanced up at the TV. "Look," he said, shifting his focus to the TV. "Can you believe what that reporter just said?" he asked, changing the topic.

"Well, I guess we have lost him for the moment," Andrea continued, looking at Jessie and laughing.

"What we just saw is a great example of the same type of thing that happens with our students, so many interruptions and shifts in focus. All of these constant distractions that our students are used to are issues we need to think about when we are preparing our instruction. I think all of us have become accustomed to information-rich, rapidly changing messages. We just don't seem to focus on one idea for very long."

"So maybe we all have changed," Andrea said thoughtfully. "Perhaps this change is something we should discuss in our PLC over the next few weeks."

"That is a great idea," Jessie agreed. "Let's examine factors that impact student retention of information and ways we can structure lessons to increase student knowledge growth."

Teaching Digital Natives

Lesson preparation is an important area where coaches might need to provide additional support. To be effective, coaches need to know how to construct instruction to meet the needs of twenty-first-century learners; content knowledge is not enough for creating an effective lesson. The National Governors Association (2005) determined that out of 10,500 high school students, more than a third of them stated that their school had not done a good job challenging them to analyze problems and think critically. In one Gallup poll (2004) of eight hundred thirteen- to seventeen-year-old students, nearly half of the students chose the adjectives *bored* and *tired* to describe their school experience. We need to engage our students in their academic content to better address their learning needs.

Task Switching

Rideout, Foehr, and Roberts (2010) found that eight- to eighteen-year-olds spent an average of seven hours each day engaged with multiple forms of digital media. Consequently, these digital natives have learned to switch their attention quickly among different sources of information, and they tend to view themselves as effective multitaskers. However, instead of multitasking, they are actually task switching (Sousa, 2011). Research has indicated that our genetic predisposition allows us to focus on only one cognitive task at a time. "The brain cannot multitask. It can focus on only one task at a time. Alternating between tasks always incurs a loss" (Sousa, 2011, p. 31). Task switching occurs at the cost of losing some of the information that was in working memory. Medina (2008) found that a person who was interrupted while they were completing a task could take up to 50 percent longer to complete the task, and that errors in the task could increase by as much as 50 percent.

Complex Texts

However, task switching and its impact on working memory and attention span are not the only factors impacting student learning. ACT (2006) conducted research to examine high school students' readiness for college and career reading. They found that the factor that most impacted reading performance was not a specific skill like identifying the main idea or cause and effect; the main factor that determined differences in reading scores was the ability to read complex texts that contained high-level vocabulary, complicated grammatical constructions, and meanings at the literal and inferred levels.

Bauerlein (2011) suggested three activities that should be encouraged to help students to be more successful with complex texts: (1) Students need to be willing to pause and deliberate over the text rather than quickly moving over the material. (2) They need opportunities for uninterrupted thinking to hold the information in working memory. Understanding complex texts requires focused attention, rather than task switching.

(3) Students also need an openness to decide whether to agree or disagree with the author and to reflect on the consequences of each position.

Technology is not evil; instead, it provides some wonderful opportunities. The challenge is providing a balance between digital and print options in such a way as to increase students' engagement and understanding, while still allowing for the reflection and sustained attention needed to comprehend complex texts. Consequently, we, as teachers, need to do a better job of using print and digital resources to help our students to become more complex thinkers.

Use of Novelty

Novelty is one way we can do this. The brain is "constantly scanning its environment for stimuli" (Sousa, 2011, p. 29). So to increase student engagement and content retention, teachers need to be able to provide novelty through the use of varied instructional materials and approaches. Some suggestions for increasing novelty might be to include humor, movement, multisensory instruction, games, and music in your instruction.

Use of Humor

Humor, as we discussed in chapter 3, has both physiological and psychological benefits. It provides more oxygen to the bloodstream, causes the release of endorphins, decreases stress and blood pressure, and relaxes muscle tension (Sousa, 2011, p. 68). Psychologically, humor helps to get and focus attention, creates a positive learning climate, increases retention and recall, improves mental health, and improves classroom management by decreasing hostility (Sousa, 2011, p. 68–69).

Use of Movement

Incorporating movement is helpful because increased activity increases the blood flow to our brains. Within a minute, there is about 15 percent more blood in the brain than there was before. Multisensory instruction that includes colorful visuals and appropriate technology increases attention and engagement. Opportunities to walk and talk about what students or teachers are learning increase retention. Games provide enjoyment and competition while also encouraging learners to manipulate and practice the concepts being taught. Music helps to increase retention of information because it is an effective memory device (Sousa, 2011).

Lesson Preparation

As we discussed, the purpose of instruction is to take information from short-term memory and move it into long-term memory. If the information is of little value, it does not make the transfer to long-term memory, so it is forgotten. Later it will be difficult to retrieve the information because you can't remember information the brain does not retain. It is not enough for the information to make sense to the student. The content must also be meaningful. However, just because the information will be on the test does not necessarily make it meaningful to the student (Sousa, 2011).

Incorporate Digital Resources

Since birth, today's students have experienced a significantly expanded digital landscape than their teachers did while growing up (Jukes, 2008). Consequently, they are more likely to be inspired and motivated by the incorporation of various forms of technology into instruction (Granito & Chernobilsky, 2012). Today's digital natives may retain more information if it comes to them through a digital medium (Prensky, 2001).

Don't Overload Information

When planning lessons, teachers need to consider the number of isolated bits of information being presented and the length of the time for which students are being asked to remember the information. These are impacted by age and motivation (Cowan, 2010).

To increase engagement and retention the coach should help the teacher construct lessons so that students answer these questions with "Yes!" (1) Does the information make sense? (2) Does the information have meaning to me? (3) Do I know what to do with the information and why I need to know this?

CHAPTER NINE

Lesson Preparation and Teacher Evaluation Systems

The teacher evaluation frameworks all contain information about lesson preparation and planning; however, each framework does not organize the information in the same way (see table 7.1). McRel's (2012) Standard 4 (Teachers Facilitate Learning for Their Students) focuses on instructional preparation. This standard encompasses eight elements: Teachers know the ways in which learning occurs and the levels of their students. They plan instruction appropriate for their students, use a variety of instructional methods, and integrate and use technology. Teachers help students develop critical-thinking and problem-solving skills, work in teams, and develop leadership qualities. They teach students to communicate effectively and support instruction by using various learning styles and a variety of methods to access the instructional content (p. 27–30). It is important that the new content knowledge is presented in a logical format, so the students are able to place their newly gained knowledge in the appropriate general and specific schemata in their long-term memory.

Content knowledge was covered in the first point of Danielson's (2013) Domain 1, which we discussed in chapter 8. The rest of Domain 1 (Planning and Preparation) focuses on instructional preparation. The remaining elements include Knowing Students, Setting Instructional Outcomes, Choosing Appropriate Resources, Designing Coherent Instruction, and Designing Student Assessments (p. 11–29).

All of Marzano's (2013) Domain 2 focuses on Planning and Preparation. The elements in this domain include Preparing for Lessons and Units, Choosing Resources and Technology, Meeting the Needs of English Language Learners, and Meeting the Needs of Students Receiving Special Education (p. 2).

Preparation for instruction is covered in the remaining section of Marshall's (2011) Domain A: Planning and Preparation for Learning. The area of content knowledge was covered in previous chapters. The rest of the domain includes Planning for Standards, Units, and Assessments, Developing Anticipation, Creating Lessons, Increasing Engagement, Choosing Materials, Differentiating Instruction, and Designing the Learning Environment (p. 2).

Without an understanding about how students learn, teachers are unable to plan effectively for instruction. Planning with others is one of the

CHAPTER NINE

most effective ways to plan instruction. This allows you to share ideas and discuss alternate strategies for accomplishing the student learning goals.

Professional Learning Communities

Professional learning communities (PLCs) are ways for teachers to work together to plan and prepare for instruction and to analyze their instructional practices through formal and informal means of data collection. DuFour and Eaker (1998) went as far as to state, "The most promising strategy for sustained, substantive school improvement is developing the ability of school personnel to function as professional learning communities" (p. xi). PLCs need to embrace a shared mission, vision, and values built on the collective inquiry process of reflection, as well as shared meaning, planning, and coordinated action (Senge et al., 1994). These steps lead to an action-oriented focus for continuous improvement (DuFour & Eaker, 1998) with the ultimate goal of improving students' academic performance.

PLC meetings provide an opportunity to discuss the content, students, instructional goals and resources, and the design and assessment of the instruction. The goal of the PLC meeting is to address the needs of individual students and teachers. With PLCs the shift is from *What am I teaching?* to *What are my students learning?* Although the frequency and length of time PLCs meet differ from location to location, the idea is that five to seven teachers meet together regularly with the goal of examining specific instructional practices. These practices are analyzed based on student learning data. Teachers then work together to identify and implement new practices and collect data to continue to increase students' learning.

Keys to Effective Coaching

The Literacy Coach Clearinghouse, PBWorks, and MIWorks indicated the importance of the coach demonstrating effective classroom and teacher relationships (see table 9.1). But we have not taken the time to look more specifically at the competencies and skills needed in this area. During teacher preparation programs, teachers receive much information about ways to provide content instruction, but the development of teacher

CHAPTER NINE

Table 9.1. Importance of Relationship Skills

Category	Self-Assessment (Literacy Coach Clearinghouse, 2009)	Coaching Characteristics (PBWorks, 2007)	Leadership Survey (MIWorks, n.d.)
Classroom and Teacher Relationships	Classroom Coaching	Relationship Skills	Interpersonal Communication

relationships is often overlooked. However, these relationship skills are probably one of the most important skills the coach needs. Each resource indicates that relationship skills are important, but what relationship skills does a coach need to develop?

Listening Skills

We are constantly hearing and processing conversation and environmental noises. But hearing is not the same as listening. Listening is the ability to accurately process and interpret auditory messages. Without this ability communication is ineffective and the message is lost. Adults spend about 75 percent of their time engaged in some sort of communication and approximately 45 percent of that time is spent listening while only 30 percent of it is spent speaking. The other 25 percent is divided between reading and writing (SkillsYouNeed.com, 2015). "The most important single skill involved in communication is the act of listening" (Hasbrouck & Denton, 2005, p. 34). According to Kimsey-House, Kimsey-House, and Sandahl (2011), listening occurs at three levels: internal, focused, and global.

Level 1: Internal Listening

This level of listening focuses on hearing your own internal voice. At this level, you are aware of the words the other person is speaking, but you are more concerned about your own opinions, stories, feelings, and needs. You may be agreeing with the other person externally, but inside you are thinking about your own topics or planning what you will say next. This happens in many situations in our lives, but when it happens in a coaching situation we can miss important information.

Level 2: Focused Listening

When you listen at this level, your attention is completely on the other person—no matter what else is happening. The world outside of the immediate conversation does not exist. You are focused not only on the actual words but also on the tone, mood, and every nuance of the conversation. At this level you are suspending any judgments and opinions. You are listening not just with words but also with your body language. Egan (1994) refers to this as an "intensity of presence" (p. 91). Hasbrouck and Denton (2005) developed the "acronym SOLER (sit squarely, open posture, leaning forward, eye contact, relaxed)" (p. 33) to describe the microskills used in focused listening. To enhance focused listening, try to arrange the space so that there are no obstacles between the two of you. In addition, try to avoid crossing your arms or legs so that your posture and gestures convey to the other person that you are open to his ideas. "In the North-American culture, a slight inclination toward a person is often seen as saying, 'I'm with you, I'm interested in you and in what you have to say'" (p. 92). Eye contact also helps to convey interest. Bolton (1979) refers to the importance of listening with "relaxed alertness," which indicates that you are comfortable but also that you are caring and attentive.

Level 3: Global Listening

Listening at this level takes in everything. You are aware of the conversation, but you are also aware of the energy between you and others, the environment, and what is going on in the environment. On this level, you are aware of the underlying mood, the tone, and the impact of the conversation. It is listening at this level that allows you to pick up as much information as possible about all the factors that are affecting the current situation.

The most effective coaching occurs when you are listening at levels 2 and 3. At level 1 the coach might be so busy evaluating his performance, the way he words his responses, and so on, that he misses other important information. Our goal as coaches is to listen at levels 2 and 3; however, it is important to be aware of when you have moved back to level 1 so that you can refocus your listening. While you are listening, you can also use silence to encourage the sharing of additional information.

CHAPTER NINE

Use of Silence

Silence plays an important role when you are listening effectively. Those pauses in the conversation can help you, as a coach, to determine the mood or feelings of the other person. Silence gives the other person an opportunity to think about or process what you have just said or asked. In addition, it gives the person time to formulate a response.

Silence is an important tool. Becoming comfortable with silence is an important first step for coaches. You can start by practicing using silence in your social conversations. Your silence allows and encourages others to talk more. If the other individual does not respond quickly to your question, don't immediately reword it. Instead, wait a short period of time before clarifying to allow the person time to think about your question. Waiting for a little while after the person responds allows the other person the opportunity to expand on his ideas. You might need to allow for even more time if the question you asked was particularly challenging or thought-provoking. During the time you are waiting, try to determine what is not being said as well as what is being said (Personal-Coaching-Information.com, 2013b).

Minimal Encouragers

Bolton (1979) identified "minimal encouragers" that can be used to indicate that you are following what the other person is saying. These encouragers could be verbal or nonverbal. Nonverbal encouragers would include things like nodding your head or smiling. Verbal ones would include responses like "I see," "Oh?" and "Really?"

Verbal Listening Skills

Verbal listening skills sound like a contradiction, but these would include such activities as reflecting, paraphrasing, and summarizing. Reflecting involves acknowledging the emotions or feelings of the speaker without commenting on the validity of those feelings or actions. Paraphrasing is restating the essence of the other's ideas in a brief or concise fashion, while summarizing would be briefly stating the important themes or issues (Hasbrouck & Denton, 2005).

CHAPTER NINE

Questioning

Questioning is another skill that is an important tool in the coach's toolbox because questions play an essential role in coaching. Questions can be planned or spontaneous. Especially during planned coaching sessions, it can be helpful to think through your goals for the session and determine ahead of time what questions you might ask. As you are constructing these questions, remember that effective questions tend to focus on what or how. Why questions can generate a lot of information, but they can also make people defensive. Why questions can sometimes be perceived as confrontational or critical (Personal-Coaching-Information.com, 2013a). After asking a question, make sure to use silence by allowing wait time for the response so that you are not the one providing the answer. Your goal is to find out what the person you are coaching knows about the problem.

To get the most out of your questions consider using open-ended rather than closed questions. Questions that are long can be confusing. Try to limit your questions to about seven words or fewer so that they are concise and easy to process. The goal for your questions is to help the person work through the situation so that she identifies the solution to the problem. Deeper learning and understanding can result from the use of clearly constructed questions. Questions can help lead to a deepening of the learning related to the specific goal. Inquiry can be used to identify the issue, gather information or data, determine next steps, implement, and evaluate the situation (Goals and Achievement, 2015).

Using Questions in the Coaching Session

Identifying the teacher's concern is an important first step in any coaching session. The teacher will be more receptive if you specifically address her issues. How you begin the coaching session is a critical step that can be the difference between success and failure. During this time it is important to do everything you can to make the teacher feel comfortable. Constructing a list of questions might help you plan for the coaching session and allow you to gather the needed information for developing an action plan (Goals and Achievement, 2015).

Some possible questions you might want to consider when beginning the session would be: What is the problem? What is making this situation difficult for you? What seems to be the main barriers to _____? What would you like to accomplish?

After the main concern has been identified, you might need to gather additional information. Again, it might be helpful to have a list of questions to use at this juncture in the session. These questions could possibly include: Tell me more about_____. What do you mean by _____? Are there any other barriers to _____? What have you tried so far?

In order to ensure that the coaching session is more than a gripe session, it is important to move the session toward a plan or resolution. Some questions you might use at this juncture would be: What do you think would be your next step? What is your plan for _____? What might be other issues you should consider?

After the problem is identified, then the plan needs to be developed so that it can be implemented. Questions to use during this final planning step might be: In what time frame do you want to accomplish this? With what frequency should this happen? How will you know that you have accomplished this? These questions can help to guide you through the coaching process (Goals and Achievement, 2015).

Faculty development through coaching is about moving new information related to teachers' concerns from short- to long-term memory. It requires focused concentration supported by modeling and practice. Listening and questioning provide the foundation for helping coaches determine how to meet teachers' needs most effectively.

Reflect and Apply Activities

9.1. Observe a conversation between two individuals. Decide whether they are listening at level 1, 2, or 3. What specific data did you use to determine the listening level?

9.2. In a conversation intentionally apply the SOLER skills (sit squarely, open posture, leaning forward, eye contact, relaxed). Did these seem to help the other person be more open in their sharing? Why or why not?

9.3. We use silence and minimal encouragers in our everyday conversations. Observe a conversation, and discuss the use of silence and minimal observers you notice.

CHAPTER NINE

References

ACT. (2006). *Reading between the lines: What the ACT reveals about readiness in reading.* Iowa City, IA: Author.

Bauerlein, M. (2011). Too dumb for complex tasks? *Educational Leadership, 68,* 28–32.

Bolton, R. (1979). *People skills: How to assert yourself, listen to others, and resolve conflicts.* New York: Simon & Schuster.

Cowan, N. (2010). The magical mystery of four: How is working memory capacity limited and why? *Current Directions in Psychological Science, 19,* 51–57.

Danielson Group. (2013). *The framework.* DanielsonGroup.org. Retrieved from https://danielsongroup.org/framework/.

DuFour, R., & Eaker, R. (1998). *Professional learning communities at work: Best practices for enhancing student achievement.* Bloomington, IN: Solution Tree Press.

Egan, G. (1994). *The skilled helper: A problem management approach to helping* (5th ed.). Pacific Grove, CA: Brooks/Cole.

Gallup. (2004). *Most teens associate school with boredom, fatigue.* Retrieved from http://www.gallup.com/poll.

Goals and Achievements. (2015). *The eight key skills for effective coaching.* Retrieved from http://goalsandachievements.com/coaching/the-8-key-skills-for-effective-coaching/.

Granito, M., & Chernobilsky, E. (2012). The effect of technology on a student's motivation and knowledge retention. *NERA Conference Proceedings,* Paper 17. Retrieved from http://digitalcommons.uconn.edu/cgi/viewcontent.cgi?article=1016&context=nera_2012.

Hasbrouck, J., & Denton, C. (2005). *The reading coach: A how-to manual for success.* Longmont, CO: Sopris West.

Jukes, I. (2008). *Understanding digital kids (DKs): Teaching and learning in the new digital landscape.* The InfoSavvy Group. Retrieved from https://pdfs.semanticscholar.org/c320/ab40afe340839998c34c866372a5b4706fc5.pdf.

Kimsey-House, H., Kimsey-House, K., & Sandahl, P. (2011). *Co-active coaching: Changing business, transforming lives* (3rd ed.). Boston, MA: Nicholas Brealey.

Literacy Coach Clearinghouse. (2009). *Self-assessment of elementary literacy coaches.* Retrieved from http://www.literacycoachingonline.org/briefs/tools/self_assessment_for_elem_lit_coaches.pdf.

Marshall, K. (2011). *Teacher evaluation rubrics.* Retrieved from http://usny.nysed.gov/rttt/teachers-leaders/practicerubrics/Docs/MarshallTeacherRubric.pdf.

Marzano, R. J. (2013). *The Marzano teacher evaluation model.* MarzanoResearch.com. Retrieved from http://tpep-wa.org/wp-content/uploads/Marzano_Teacher_Evaluation_Model.pdf.

McRel. (2012). *North Carolina teacher evaluation process.* Retrieved from http://www.uncfsu.edu/Documents/soe/assessment/teach-eval-manual.pdf.

Medina, J. (2008). *Brain rules.* Seattle, WA: Pear Press.

MIWorks.org. (n.d.). *Leadership self-assessment.* Retrieved from http://miworks.org/virtualcareerlab/Effective%20Leadership/Leadership%20Self%20Assessment.pdf.

National Governors Association. (2005). *Rate your future survey.* Washington, DC: Author. Retrieved from http://www.nga.org.

PBWorks. (2007). *Becoming an effective coach.* Retrieved from http://coaches.pbworks.com/w/page/7518652/Becoming%20an%20Effective%20Coach#CharacteristicsofEffectiveCoaches.

Personal-Coaching-Information.com. (2013a). *Open coaching questions.* Retrieved from http://www.personal-coaching-information.com/open-coaching-questions.html.

Personal-Coaching-Information.com. (2013b). *Use of silence—a powerful coaching skill.* Retrieved from http://www.personal-coaching-information.com/use-of-silence.html.

Prensky, M. (2001, October). Digital natives, digital immigrants. *On the Horizon, 9*(5). Retrieved from http://www.marcprensky.com/writing/Prensky%20-%20Digital%20Natives,%20Digital%20Immigrants%20-%20Part1.pdf.

Rideout, V. J., Foehr, U. G., & Roberts, D. F. (2010). *Generation M2: Media in the lives of 8- to 18- year-olds.* Menlo Park, CA: Kaiser Family Foundation.

Senge, P., Kleiner, A., Roberts, C., Ross, R. B., & Smith, B. J. (1994). *The fifth dimension field book: Strategies and tools for building a learning organization.* New York: Currency.

SkillsYouNeed.com. (2015). *Listening skills.* Retrieved from http://www.skillsyouneed.com/ips/listening-skills.html.

Sousa, D. A. (2011). *How the brain learns* (4th ed.). Thousand Oaks, CA: Corwin.

CHAPTER TEN

Jessie grabbed her phone and her folders from the desk. She had two PLCs this afternoon. The first one was with the fifth-grade team. And, of course, it was at the other end of the school from Jan Morrison's second-grade class, where she had just been helping her analyze the progress-monitoring data from the first assessment period. The e-mail she had received from Max Milford, the fifth-grade team leader, had said that they were going to be discussing "classroom environment."

Jessie greeted Max and Heather Raymore as she entered the classroom. The meeting was just about to get started, so she took the seat beside Lauren Prentus and John Concord. Max started the discussion. "I asked Jessie to come to share some ideas about evaluating classroom environments because last time there was some general discussion about what that term actually meant."

"I can see why you were discussing classroom environment," Jessie commented. "With the new evaluation system we are using, classroom environment is being evaluated much more specifically than it has been before."

"On the previous evaluation forms," John commented, "in fact, for all the twenty-five years that I have been teaching, it was not even a part of the evaluation system."

"Yes, you are right, John," agreed Jessie. "But at least the new evaluation system spells out exactly what is involved in classroom environment."

CHAPTER TEN

"So what exactly are we talking about?" Lauren asked. "I haven't had a chance to look at the information. Is it the physical, social, or instructional environment?"

"Great question. If the major emphasis is student achievement, which of those do you think would be important?" Jessie asked.

"Well," John started, "certainly not the physical environment. No one cares if the desks are in a row."

"Actually," Heather commented, entering the conversation, "when I arrange my desks in groups it makes it easier for me to have my students talk to each other, so I would think they all would be important."

"Heather," Jessie continued, "that seems to be what I am seeing too, when I look at the forms. It seems to be all three. Let's brainstorm a list of characteristics related to the physical, social, and cultural environment that would be important to consider. I can write down your ideas here on the board, and we can compare them to the form I brought. Then you could use your list or the form I brought to help you evaluate your own classroom environment."

"But how do I know if I am interpreting each point in the same way someone else will?" Lauren asked.

"That is a great question. Does anyone have any ideas?" Jessie asked.

"We can't be in anyone else's room since we all have planning at the same time. Otherwise we would not be able to meet for the PLC," Lauren continued.

"You seem to have a great idea about watching each other. Maybe you would find it helpful to pair up and observe each other's class, and I could cover your class for a little while as you observe each other," Jessie suggested. "You have come up with some great ideas about how you can work together to support each other. See what items you want to put on your classroom environment list. I have to go to the third-grade PLC, but after you pair up let me know what times would work best for you and when you would like me to cover your class so you can observe each other."

Classroom Environment

The classroom environment is an important multifaceted component of instruction, as evidenced by each of the teacher evaluation systems. All four of the teacher evaluation systems focus on the importance of the physical,

CHAPTER TEN

social/cultural, and academic environments. Coaches can work with teachers to help create effective classroom environments. Danielson's (2013) Domain 2: Classroom Environment, Marshall's (2011) Domain B: Classroom Management, and Marzano's (2013) Domain 1: Classroom Strategies and Behaviors elements 1–5 and 24–41 all specifically discuss the classroom environment and practices. In the McRel (2012) evaluation system, elements of the classroom environment are discussed throughout the domains rather than being located in one specific domain. The inclusion of the classroom environment in all the teacher evaluation systems illustrates its importance.

Many factors impact the classroom environment. When working with a teacher to refine the classroom environment, it might be helpful for the coach to have a document that can be shared with the teacher. The form in appendix H, Environmental Observation Form, could be used to help facilitate a discussion about various aspects of the classroom environment.

Physical Environment

A classroom is more than just the instructional practices. In the scenario above, John made the observation that the physical environment was not important; however, there are many components of the physical environment. The first things to consider would be basic characteristics such as cleanliness, light, and temperature.

Lighting

The amount and type of lighting is an important consideration. Jago and Tanner (1999) indicated that lighting is one of the most critical physical factors in a classroom. Students, especially those with vision challenges, find it easier to focus in well-lit settings than in poorly lit ones. As you examine the room, determine whether there is enough light; however, also consider whether the lighting creates a glare on the paper or board, making it difficult to read.

Not only is the amount of light a consideration, but the type of light bulbs is also important. Choi and Suk (2016) further investigated the impact of classroom lighting on academic performance using tunable LED lights. The researchers concluded that the 3500 K warm lighting may provide a relaxing environment to support recess activities, whereas the 5000 K "standard" lighting may be applied for reading activities, and 6500 K dynamic lighting supports students' performance during intensive academic activities such as standardized assessments. They further observed that lighting in educational facilities was "much poorer than they anticipated" (Howard, 2016, para. 5).

Noise

Noise level is another important consideration. Noise created by students' interactions and movement throughout the room is unavoidable. However, the room should still be generally quiet enough for the students to be able to work independently or in small groups as needed. Various classroom activities require differing noise levels. The background noise level for group work will be different from that needed for silent reading. There are many different ways to monitor the noise level in the room.

Various programs are available for monitoring noise levels. Bouncy Balls (https://bouncyballs.org/) is a program that works directly with your computer and built in microphone. Simply turn your microphone on and as the noise level increases the visual bubble display becomes more active. The program offers a variety of different visual displays such as bubbles, balls, eyes, and faces and can be projected to provide visual support for managing classroom noise level.

Temperature

Room temperature is another important factor; however, it is sometimes outside of the teacher's control. It is difficult for students to concentrate on their work if they are too hot or too cold. If the teacher cannot control the temperature, students should be encouraged to dress in layers so they can add or subtract layers as needed. Perez, Montano, and Perez (2015) found that when the same assessment was offered to different classes, classes in rooms with controlled temperatures had higher mean scores than the mean scores of classroom that were too warm (81 degrees) or too cold (61 degrees).

Room Arrangement

The physical arrangement of the room can impact learning. The specific grade level will determine the students' physical needs. Room dividers should be low enough to allow the teacher visibility of the entire room. Areas for group work should be located away from the areas where students will be working quietly. Classroom arrangements that allow for students to easily interact with their peers will more readily encourage collaboration (Teacher Vision, 2015).

Traffic Flow

The general classroom layout should allow for an ease of traffic flow. This is particularly important if the class includes students with physical challenges such as wheelchairs or crutches. Classroom routines is an area that could be addressed in both the physical and the instructional environment. Students should be knowledgeable about the routines, and the space should be arranged so that students can implement these routines easily. This would include submitting assignments and distributing work.

Electrical cords, piles of books or papers, and general clutter can make navigation around the room difficult. Make sure that movement around the room is not impeded. Be particularly cognizant of electrical cords or area rugs that can cause a tripping hazard.

Visual Displays

The arrangement of information on the walls is another important consideration. Bulletin boards, posters, and other information should relate to the current unit of study. "Effective teachers treat classroom walls as creative palettes for designing both aesthetically pleasing, but also instructionally useful displays of instructional information" (Reutzel & Cooter, 2012, p. 16).

Displays should incorporate student work. These work displays provide a sample of quality projects, while increasing student ownership (Teacher Vision, 2015).

Social/Cultural Environment

Today's classrooms are becoming more and more diverse; consequently, an important dimension of effective instruction is the recognition of this cultural diversity. Diverse cultural experiences can strengthen academic

CHAPTER TEN

learning (Reutzel & Cooter, 2012). An inclusive classroom values the contribution that each child brings through his unique language, culture, interests, and identity. There are numerous characteristics that exemplify the socially and culturally diverse classroom.

Teacher–Student Interactions

In effective classrooms, the interactions between the teacher and the students are calm and supportive. The general classroom atmosphere is warm and inviting (Gray, 2012). Teachers exemplify appropriate interpersonal communication and interaction through modeling responsible behavior (Tompkins, 2010). The teacher's interactions with students are caring and accepting, and the teacher demonstrates a concern for students' emotional and academic growth.

Research has supported the importance of this relationship. High levels of emotional support are associated with growth in reading and math achievement from kindergarten through fifth grade (Pianta et al., 2008). This same pattern was evident in the secondary classroom. When teacher–student interactions were emotionally and intellectually engaging to adolescents, achievement test performance gains for the average student rose from the thirty-fifth to the sixtieth percentile (Center for Advanced Study of Teaching and Learning, n.d.).

Peer Interactions

Peer interactions between students are supportive and calm. Students feel safe because they know they will not be bullied, but instead will be accepted by their classmates. Learning, as a process of taking risks and exploring ideas, is encouraged (Tompkin, 2010). Modeling and instructional routines are used to teach students how to appropriately discuss topics with one another (Reutzel & Cooter, 2012).

Respect Is Evident

There is an attitude of respect and rapport within the classroom (Dusenbury, 2015). Students demonstrate that they respect others, the teacher, and their school by their comments and the appropriate treatment of resources. Students are willing to provide support when needed

CHAPTER TEN

by either the students or the teacher. The teacher and the students "work together for their common good" (Tompkins, 2010, p. 16).

Student Expectations Clearly Stated

Expected, acceptable behavior is clearly described; however, classroom rules might or might not be posted depending on the age of the students and the time of the year. Even if the rules are not posted, the students know the classroom rules because the teacher has set the expectations and communicated these to the students. The classroom rules are specific and consistent and demonstrated through teacher modeling and reinforcement (Tompkins, 2010).

Multicultural Materials Used

Materials reflect students' cultural background. Materials should reflect the cultures, races, and ethnicities in the classroom, as well as those not represented, even if the classroom is not culturally diverse. Multicultural literature is used to develop cross-cultural awareness and appreciation. "Culturally responsive classrooms empower all students, including those from marginalized groups, to become more successful readers and writers" (Tompkins, 2010, p. 9). Instruction that is culturally responsive acknowledges students' cultures and social customs and teaches appreciation of others' heritages.

Classroom Management

Classroom disruptions are handled calmly. In every classroom there will be disruptions. These can be as simple as a fire drill or as serious as a fight or injury. By identifying best possible ways for handling situations, the teacher is prepared to handle disruptions when they occur. Partin (2005) supported this observation by stating, "When you lose your composure in front of the class, they, not you, are in control of your behavior" (p. 26).

When developing the social/cultural environment, teachers should attempt to make all students feel comfortable. It is difficult for children to learn when they are concerned about physical needs, safety, belonging, or esteem (Huitt, 2007). Teachers should have high expectations for all learners (New Zealand Department of Education, 2015). In a socially and culturally supportive classroom, the teacher realizes that all students can learn and adjusts instruction as needed to accomplish this.

Instructional Environment

The instructional environment refers to the strategies, materials, and routines used within the classroom. Research has linked positive academic environments to higher student test scores and increased graduation rates (American Institutes for Research, 2015).

Organization

Research supports the importance of teacher and classroom organization. In fact, high levels of classroom organization were found to be associated with gains in first graders' literacy (Ponitz, Rimm-Kaufman, Brock, & Nathanson, 2016). The instructional materials should be organized and readily available. The materials that the teacher needs for the lesson are within easy reach so that instruction is not interrupted while materials are being retrieved, organized, or distributed.

Student Involvement

Students are actively involved in the instruction. Students participate in the lesson and have opportunities to reflect and to teach and learn from others. Opportunities to talk with peers and work collaboratively are provided (Tompkins, 2010).

Differentiation

Differentiation and/or modifications are incorporated regularly into instructional practices. In effective classrooms, the teacher realizes that all students do not learn in the same way, through the same methods and examples, or at the same rate. Lessons are differentiated to meet the students' needs.

Differentiation occurs through the use of various types of instructional groupings. The teacher realizes that whole-group instruction is not always the most effective method for lesson presentation. The teacher determines when appropriate to use whole-group, small-group, partners, or individual instruction at different times throughout the instructional sequence.

Different modalities of presentation are used as opposed to a dependence predominantly on auditory presentation. Research indicates that lecturing is an ineffective instructional approach (Eggen & Kauchak, 2010). Presenting content information through visual, auditory, and kinesthetic methods helps to address different learners' strengths and serves to increase the connections made within the brain.

Transitions

Transitions between topics occur smoothly. Transitions can be a difficult time because students are more easily distracted when changing activities. Students should understand the general classroom routines and procedures so that instruction is not disrupted during the transitions. Establishing routines that are predictable and familiar enables students to feel comfortable, safe, and willing to take risks (Tompkins, 2010).

Student Achievement Is Valued

Learning and growth are valued. Teachers provide explicit, scaffolded instruction through modeling and guided and independent practice. Students' learning and growth is recognized and rewarded (Tompkins, 2010). Students show pride in their work. As a result of what is happening in the classroom, students are proud of what they are accomplishing.

Providing Feedback after an Observation

In your role as the coach, you helped a teacher plan a lesson, and then you had the opportunity to observe that lesson. Now it is time for the feedback session. This session is a time to discuss what happened during the lesson and to set goals for future lessons based on the assessment data. The process is similar no matter what the instructional level; however, the starting point or emphasis may change depending on the grade level where the teacher provides instruction.

CHAPTER TEN

Grade-Level Concerns

At the middle and high school content area level, it might be more effective to begin the discussion by focusing on the content rather than focusing on literacy skills or behavior first. Secondary teachers tend to view themselves as content experts and view instruction through the lens of the one specific content they teach. For example, if you observed a science lesson, teacher buy-in might be increased through beginning the discussion by focusing on the science content. However, to be able to discuss this perspective, the coach needs to have a thorough understanding of the content area standards and concepts (Puig & Froelich, 2007).

Elementary teachers, on the other hand, because they typically teach many different content areas, tend to focus more on teaching strategies, and they have a more interdisciplinary approach to teaching.

Setting the Teacher at Ease

In an attempt to set the teacher at ease, it might be helpful to begin with an example of a time a second set of eyes has helped you address students' concerns. This type of an approach helps to reassure the teacher that you are focusing on student achievement, not on evaluating their teaching.

Teacher Respect

During the conversation, try to find out whether the teacher was surprised by anything that happened during the lesson. It would also be helpful to know whether the day you observed was a "typical" day. Don't try to give too much feedback at once. Structure your feedback like an Oreo. Begin by discussing effective positive aspects of the lesson. Then choose only one or two areas where the teacher might want to change. Everything can't be addressed at once. Finish the discussion with a few positive comments. Remember to convey respect for the teacher as a professional (Hasbrouck & Denton, 2005).

Structuring Feedback

As you structure your feedback conference, remembering these points might make your feedback sessions go more smoothly.

CHAPTER TEN

1. First, and most important, your role is coaching, not supervisory.
2. Your ultimate goal is to improve students' academic skills and competence, not to evaluate the teacher's teaching.
3. If the teacher has concerns, engage the teacher in systematic problem solving to find ways to support students' academic growth.
4. Limit your observations to student behaviors that are relevant to learning.
5. Try to provide at least three points of positive feedback that reinforce effective aspects of the lesson.
6. Identify only one or two important areas where the teacher might want to consider changes. The teacher can focus on only a few things at a time.

The classroom environment is a multifaceted topic. The teacher's and coach's goal is to work together to create a setting where students feel free to take risks as they are growing in their skills and understanding academically, socially, and emotionally. Teachers are responsible for creating that environment for their students. Coaches can provide another set of eyes to help the teacher to see the environment from a different perspective. The Environmental Observation Form (appendix H) can help the coach to start a conversation about this important aspect of teaching.

Reflect and Apply Activities

10.1. Teacher evaluation systems throughout the nation are changing. Examine the evaluation system your district is currently using and identify in which sections of the evaluation system the classroom environment is assessed.

10.2. Use Domain 2 of Danielson's framework to evaluate the learning environment of a lesson you have observed in person or online. Identify strengths and areas for growth.

CHAPTER TEN

10.3. Observe a lesson either in person or online. Using the Environmental Observation Form as a basis, write or record a feedback conference that could be used to provide feedback to the teacher. Remember to provide positive feedback but also to identify a couple of suggestions for further refinement of the teacher's instructional practices.

References

American Institutes for Research. (2015). *Instructional environment*. Safe Supportive Learning. Retrieved from http://safesupportivelearning.ed.gov/topic-research/environment/instructional-environment.

Bouncy Balls. (2015). Retrieved from https://bouncyballs.org/.

Center for Advanced Study of Teaching and Learning. (n.d.). *Measuring and improving teacher–student interactions in PK–12 settings to enhance students' learning*. Retrieved from http://curry.virginia.edu/uploads/resourceLibrary/CLASS-MTP_PK-12_brief.pdf.

Choi, K., & Suk, H. (2016). Dynamic lighting system for the learning environment: Performance of elementary students. *The Optics Express*, 24(10), 907–16. Retrieved from https://www.osapublishing.org/oe/abstract.cfm?uri=oe-24-10-A907.

Danielson Group. (2013). *The framework*. DanielsonGroup.org. Retrieved from https://danielsongroup.org/framework/.

Dusenbury, L. (2015). *Creating a safe classroom environment*. Education World. Retrieved from http://www.educationworld.com/a_curr/creating-safe-classroom-environment-climate.shtml.

Eggen, P., & Kauchak, D. (2010). *Educational psychology: Windows on classrooms* (8th ed.). Upper Saddle River, NJ: Merrill/Prentice Hall.

Gray, S. (2012). 5 Ways to create a culturally responsive classroom. *Infinite Hope*. The National Equity Project blog. Retrieved from https://blog.nationalequityproject.org/2012/08/22/5-ways-to-create-a-culturally-responsive-classroom/.

Hasbrouck, J., & Denton, C. (2005). *The reading coach: A how-to manual for success*. Longmont, CO: Sopris West.

Howard, J. (2016, April 29). How just the right lighting may improve learning in classrooms. *Huffington Post*. Retrieved from http://www.huffingtonpost.com/entry/lighting-boost-learning-concentration_us_5720cb14e4b0b49df6a9b73e.

Huitt, W. (2007). Maslow's hierarchy of needs. *Educational Psychology Interactive*. Valdosta, GA: Valdosta State University. Retrieved from http://www.edpsycinteractive.org/topics/conation/maslow.html.

Jago, E., & Tanner, K. (1999). *Influence of the school facility on student achievement*. University of Georgia. Retrieved from http://sdpl.coe.uga.edu/research abstracts/visual.html.

Marshall, K. (2011). *Teacher evaluation rubrics*. Retrieved from http://usny.nysed.gov/rttt/teachers-leaders/practicerubrics/Docs/MarshallTeacherRubric.pdf.

Marzano, R. J. (2013). *The Marzano teacher evaluation model*. MarzanoResearch.com. Retrieved from http://tpep-wa.org/wp-content/uploads/Marzano_Teacher_Evaluation_Model.pdf.

McRel. (2012). North Carolina teacher evaluation process. Retrieved from http://www.uncfsu.edu/Documents/soe/assessment/teach-eval-manual.pdf.

New Zealand Department of Education. (2015). *Inclusive education guides for schools*. Author. Retrieved from http://inclusive.tki.org.nz/guides/developing-an-inclusive-classroom-culture.

Partin, R. L. (2005). *Classroom teacher's survival guide: Practical strategies, management techniques, and reproducibles for new and experienced teachers*. San Francisco, CA: Jossey-Bass.

Perez, J., Montano, J., & Perez, J. (2015). *Does temperature impact student performance?* Healthy Schools. Retrieved from http://healthyschools.cefpi.org/temperature.html.

Pianta, R., Belsky, J., Vandergrift, N., Houts, R., Morrison, F. (2008). Classroom effects on children's achievement trajectories in elementary school. *American Educational Research Journal, 45*(2), 365–97.

Ponitz, C. C., Rimm-Kaufman, S., Brock, L., & Nathanson, L. (2016). Contributions of gender, early school adjustment, and classroom organizational climate to first grade outcomes. *Elementary School Journal* [in press].

Puig, E. A., & Froelich, K. S. (2007). *The literacy coach: Guiding in the right direction*. Boston, MA: Pearson Education.

Reutzel, D. R., & Cooter, R. B. (2012). *Teaching children to read: The teacher makes the difference*. Boston, MA: Pearson Education.

Teacher Vision. (2015). *Creating an effective physical classroom environment*. Retrieved from https://www.teachervision.com/classroom-management/decorative-arts/6506.html?page=1.

Tompkins, G. E. (2010). *Literacy for the 21st century: A balanced approach* (5th ed.). Boston, MA: Allyn & Bacon.

CHAPTER ELEVEN

Jessie reflected on the meeting with the fifth-grade PLC as she hurried over to the third-grade pod. Max and Lauren had paired up right away and had, before she left, already identified a time that they wanted to observe each other. They were excited about using the Environmental Observation Tool because it included so many of the ideas the team had identified together. Heather and John were not as enthusiastic, though. John had been polite but distant, and Heather had not really said much. "I do wonder what she was thinking," mused Jessie. "Heather has only been teaching a year, and from what I hear, her class this year is really a handful."

As she reached the door of the third-grade pod, her thoughts shifted to the next meeting. Dianne, the team leader for the third-grade PLC, had indicated that they were concerned about "enhancing students' higher-order thinking skills."

"Oh, I hope I am not late. It looks like everyone is already here," Jessie commented, taking the empty seat between Dianne and Beth. "No problem. Glad you could make it."

"Rachel, would you be willing to read the notes from our last meeting, so we are all on the same page?" Dianne asked.

"Last time we looked at the scores from the reading unit tests and did an item analysis. We noticed that many of our students did not do well on the last two questions, which are the ones that required more than a literal comprehension of the passage," Rachel said, looking up

CHAPTER ELEVEN

from her notes. "That's what I have; so what are we going to do about this problem? Any thoughts?"

Beth responded, "Well, we already teach thinking skills. We ask them a lot of higher-order questions, and we model our thought process. We really can't do much else. It is just the way kids are these days."

"What does anyone else think?" Jessie asked, trying to encourage some other thoughts about the issue.

"I feel like I am asking higher-order thinking questions, but I guess now that you ask about it specifically, I am not really sure," Dianne replied thoughtfully.

"It might be interesting to see how many higher-order questions are being asked or even just to track the types of questions being asked. Since we are not really sure what is happening, this might be an interesting question to investigate," Jessie suggested. "Anybody have any ideas on how to do that?"

"There really isn't anyway to do that," Beth insisted.

"Well, maybe we could," Dianne responded. "It might be as simple as a tally sheet. If I put a small piece of paper on the table during small-group instruction, I could put a tally mark for each lower- or higher-level question I ask. I would then be able to compare the totals for each type. Then I would know how many of each type I was asking, and which type I was asking more of."

"That is way too much to keep track of," complained Beth.

"If I tried to do it for all my groups, it sure would be," Dianne agreed. "I would go insane trying to do it all day, but I think I could do it with just one of my reading groups. I would be interested in knowing this for myself. And maybe I will get my kids involved. They could help me remember, and it might actually reinforce the idea of which questions require higher-order thinking."

"So, what do you think? Shall we all try it over the next week?" Rachel suggested. "Then we can share our findings at our PLC meeting next week. We can figure out from there what we want to do. You know, as I work to fit in more questions, it might be nice to have some question stems to help generate them," she added.

"I can help you with that," Jessie volunteered. "I will get a list to you. Does that sound like it would be helpful?"

CHAPTER ELEVEN

Bloom's Taxonomy

The third-grade team was concerned about their students' ability to answer higher-order thinking questions. These higher-order questions tend to encompass the upper three levels of Bloom's taxonomy: analysis, synthesis, and evaluation.

In 1956 Bloom led a group of educational psychologists who developed a classification system for intellectual behavior. The group's original analysis resulted in the six-level taxonomy of knowledge, comprehension, application, analysis, synthesis, and evaluation. Lorin Anderson, one of Bloom's former students, recently updated the taxonomy to reflect twenty-first-century ideas (Overbaugh & Schultz, n.d.). The revised Bloom's taxonomy is still composed of six levels, but the nouns in the original classification system were renamed by verbs and the order was revised slightly. The new model is remembering, understanding, applying, analyzing, evaluating, and creating. In the original version of Bloom's taxonomy, each level encompassed the previous levels. However, the revised hierarchy allows for some overlap in the levels (Sousa, 2011).

Levels of Higher-Order Thinking

The three lower levels of Bloom's taxonomy, the lower-order thinking, focus on convergent thinking. While using thought processes at these levels, the learner takes information that is known and understood and solves problems through application of this knowledge. The upper three levels of the hierarchy, the higher-order thinking, focus on divergent thinking where the learner is discovering new ideas and insights.

Instead of just two levels of higher- and lower-order thinking, Bloom's taxonomy could also be divided into a three-tiered process. In the three-tiered model, the levels of remembering and understanding are combined as the skills needed for the acquisition of knowledge. The applying and analyzing levels are used to transform the knowledge or information. Generating new information based on the knowledge occurs at the evaluating and creating levels (Sousa, 2011). Consequently, some models view higher-order thinking as the top two levels of Bloom's taxonomy, while others include the top three levels in this process.

CHAPTER ELEVEN

Encouraging Higher-Order Thinking

Questioning is a powerful tool for helping students to better understand concepts while setting high expectations and promoting critical and creative thinking. However, before students can be successful at higher-order thinking, they must have sufficient practice with lower-level questions. The answers to these remembering and understanding questions provide information about students' preparation, and they encourage review and/or summarization of the content. Students need opportunities to apply their learning rather than just follow the teacher's example of the application; higher-order questions help to accomplish this. Higher-order questions encourage students to think deeply and critically while encouraging discussion (Buono, 2014). Questioning strategies that promote higher-order thinking require students to manipulate prior information, reword, conclude, observe, describe, compare, or contrast concepts. (See appendix I for Higher-Order Question Stems and Projects.)

To enhance student thinking, it is important that teachers avoid yes or no questions and instead focus on open-ended questions. When using higher-order questions, teachers will need to increase think and wait time to allow time for students to process information at a deeper level. Within the lesson, teachers should structure their questions so that they move from the simplest levels to the more complex. Within the classroom setting, it is important to encourage all students to be part of higher-order thinking discussions.

Thinking and Emotion

As teachers are trying to encourage higher-order thinking, it is important to remember that positive emotions tend to increase attention and enhance critical thinking. When students' responses are met with neutral and/or negative responses, this decreases attention and engagement. These are important factors to keep in mind when trying to encourage higher-order thinking. Students need to be encouraged to use the basic processes of thinking such as observing, generalizing, assessing, and forming conclusions as a basis for the higher-level thinking processes. These lower-level thinking skills form the basis for hypothesizing, inferring, and predicting.

CHAPTER ELEVEN

Difference between Complexity and Difficulty

Higher-order thinking skills require more complex thinking. However, questions can be difficult without being at a higher complexity level. Asking a student to add 2 + 2 is a knowledge-level question. Asking a student to multiply 2,354 × 8,976 is still at the knowledge level, but it is a significantly more difficult question. Examining the learner's behavior will help to identify the level of complexity in a question.

Complexity refers to the thought process needed to deal with the information. To answer complex questions, students must demonstrate thinking at higher levels of Bloom's taxonomy. Lower-level questions, even when difficult, typically have one specific answer or solution, while complex questions may have more than one possible answer. Difficulty refers to the amount of effort the learner expands within a specific level of thinking. Activities can become increasingly difficult without becoming more complex. If teachers want to increase higher-order thinking, they need to increase the level of complexity, not just the level of difficulty (Francis, 2015).

Working with Resistant Teachers

When the coach goes into the classroom or works with a group of teachers, it can be normal for teachers to experience some anxiety, even when the coach indicates she is only there to help. The teachers might assume that the coach is there because they did something wrong that needs to be fixed. Teachers with this type of an attitude perceive the coach as having a top-down leadership style.

Avoiding a Top-Down Process

There are two difficulties when coaching is perceived as a top-down process. First, the teacher might agree to the coach's suggestions only to appease the coach. In this case, the instructional changes the teacher adopts tend not to last because they are not changes the teacher has viewed as important. The teacher did not have buy-in or ownership in the change process. Instead, the changes were implemented to please someone else. Second, a top-down process does not encourage trust or confidence between the teacher and the coach.

CHAPTER ELEVEN

Another problematic approach to coaching occurs when the coach is perceived as being sent by or as a representative of the principal. Not only is this a top-down approach, but it also makes the teachers feel that the principal and the coach are teamed up against them. When this happens, the teacher might wonder what is being discussed about her behind her back. This makes it seem as though the administration has identified a problem and the coach is there to fix it. Again, this approach serves to put the teacher on the defensive and corrodes trust between the coach and the teacher.

Peer Coaching

During the third-grade PLC meeting, Beth was resistant to analyzing the higher-order questioning. Jessie did not allow herself to be drawn into an argument about whether the teachers were asking higher-level thinking questions. Instead, Jessie challenged the teachers to find the answer for themselves. There are two possible approaches Jessie could have used to handle Beth's resistant behavior: peer coaching or action research. Showers and Joyce (1996) suggest the use of peer coaching. In this approach, two teachers plan together, observe each other teaching the same lesson, and then reflect together after the lessons have been taught.

Action Research

A second possible approach, which is the one that Jessie decided to use, would be to fashion an action research project. Jessie proposed a very simple action research project to the team of third-grade teachers. The research question to be investigated was how frequently teachers asked higher-order questions. Investigating the specific question provided any resistant teachers with a means of supporting their perception that they were using higher-order questions while at the same time it provided a way to compare teachers' instructional practices with those of others.

Make Them Part of a Group

Action research is an effective way to deal with those teachers who are resistant. It makes the problem-solving approach more collaborative. Jessie did not attempt to work with Beth by herself. Instead, she encouraged Beth to be a part of a group action research project. The small-group problem-solving approach allowed the teachers to discuss together the issue they had identified. The coach facilitated the discussion about the identified topic. Then they discussed possible strategies they thought might effectively address the problem. The goal was to isolate strategies or variables that might be effective and develop a framework for implementing them in the school setting. This type of an approach takes the focus off of the resistant teacher and encourages more group collaboration.

Steps in the Action Research Process

Instituting an action research project is a great way to get teachers to try out new ideas. The group decides on one particular strategy they want to investigate with their students. The goal is to conduct classroom field tests to determine whether the technique is effective in their specific setting. Action research is a "way to create an environment of knowledgeable professionals that are equipped with the content and process to impact student achievement" (Moss, Sloan, & Sandor, 2009, p. 74). Working through this process with the coach creates a safe environment for adapting methods to reach more diverse groups of learners.

In the action research process, the group develops a plan for implementation and data collection. Baseline data is collected before strategy implementation to determine the current extent of the problem. A plan is developed in an attempt to correct the problem. Then the coach and the teachers work together to determine that there is inter-rater reliability between the teachers in the implementation, collection, and analysis of the data. This allows each of the teachers to see the strategy modeled and evaluate its implementation as well. Then the final data is collected and analyzed to determine the effect of the strategy in their specific school setting. The action research process helps to establish a collaborative environment.

Providing Support

Administration and the coach can further support the action research process in many ways. Some of these are listed below.

- They can provide additional support materials through books, videos, and other information.
- They can highlight the staff's research projects with other departments and grades.
- They can provide examples of how others have implemented action research.
- They can bring in outside experts.
- They can provide opportunities for staff to share their research with the school or other departments.

In addition, creating a running list of interesting action research projects can help get everyone thinking about research projects and how teachers can positively impact student achievement (Spaulding & Smith, 2012).

Coaches help teachers to increase their students' ability to answer more difficult and more complex questions. These complex questions use higher-order thinking skills. Action research can be used to help encourage resistant teachers to explore concerns and to seek solutions to questions about their instructional practice.

Reflect and Apply Activities

11.1. Observe a lesson online or in person and tally the number of higher- and lower-order questions. Determine what percentage of the questions are higher-order questions. Identify additional higher-order questions that could have been asked. Use appendix I to help you.

11.2. Identify an area where there is teacher resistance at your school. Develop a plan to use peer coaching to address this issue.

11.3. Identify an area where there is teacher resistance at your school, and develop an action research project to address this issue.

CHAPTER ELEVEN

References

Buono, S. (2014). *Developing higher-order thinking questions to promote student learning.* Palmyra School District. Retrieved from http://www.palmyra schools.com/ps/District%20Administration/Curriculum%20and%20 Instruction/Professional%20Development/Higher%20Order%20Thinking %20Presentation.pdf.

Francis, E. (2015). *H.O.T./D.O.K.* [blog about teaching higher-order thinking and depth of knowledge]. Retrieved from http://maverikeducation.blogspot .com/.

Moss, G., Sloan, L., & Sandor, J. (2009). Peer coaching and action research as professional development. *Writing Partnerships: Theory into Practice, 4*(2), 68–81.

Overbaugh, R. C., & Schultz, L. (n.d.). *Bloom's taxonomy.* Old Dominion University. Retrieved from http://ww2.odu.edu/educ/roverbau/Bloom/blooms_ taxonomy.htm.

Showers, B., & Joyce, B. (1996). The evolution of peer coaching. *Educational Leadership, 53,* 12–16.

Sousa, D. A. (2011). *How the brain learns* (4th ed.). Thousand Oaks, CA: Corwin.

Spaulding, D. T., & Smith, G. (2012). *Instructional coaches and the instructional leadership team: A guide for school-building improvement.* Thousand Oaks, CA: Corwin.

CHAPTER TWELVE

"Jessie," Heather said, sticking her head in the doorway after school on Thursday. "Do you have a minute?"

"Sure," Jessie said with a smile, "Come on in. I was just finishing up some paperwork. How is it going? Did you and John find a time you wanted me to cover your class?"

"Well, that is kind of what I wanted to talk to you about," Heather began hesitantly. "You know this is my first year in fifth grade, and I am finding it a little challenging."

"First years can be difficult," Jessie agreed.

"Until I feel like I have a stronger handle on my kids' behavior, I don't really want to invite anyone into my room. Do you have any suggestions I can try? I feel like my kids have the upper hand."

"That can be really frustrating; let's see what we can come up with together. Two heads are better than one. Can you tell me a little bit about how you begin class and the rules, procedures, and routines you have instituted?"

"Well," Heather began, thinking. "The kids come into the room and when the bell rings, I get their attention, and then I take roll. When we finally get the lunch count out of the way, then we start on small-group reading lessons," Heather continued.

"Is that working well for you?" Jessie questioned.

"No, to be honest, I am feeling totally frustrated. The day seems to immediately deteriorate as soon as the students enter the room in the morning," Heather complained.

CHAPTER TWELVE

"Would you like me to come into the room to observe and see if there are any suggestions I might have?" Jessie suggested. "Take a little time and decide exactly what is bothering you most and we can start there. Then based on what you identify, I could pull out some forms and we could talk about exactly how we can collect data to address what you would like to work on," Jessie continued.

"OK, let me think about it tonight and tomorrow and we can talk after school tomorrow, if that works for you," Heather said, looking a tiny bit more relieved than when she came in.

Classroom Management

As Heather discovered, managing a classroom is not always as easy as experienced teachers can make it seem. Coaches, although not behavior specialists, are often asked about how to correct behavior problems that are impacting student achievement. Because behavior impacts achievement, it can be difficult to separate the two.

Classroom management includes all the things teachers do to establish a productive working environment where students are engaged in the learning process. "Effective teachers manage their classrooms. Ineffective teachers discipline their classrooms" (Wong & Wong, 2001, p. 11). In the well-managed classroom, students are involved in their work, know what is expected, waste a minimal amount of time, and focus on their work. The classroom climate is focused yet relaxed. Effective teachers are in control of their classroom but are not obsessed with having that control. Students are empowered to make decisions about their learning (Partin, 2005).

Establishing Classroom Rules

Rules, procedures, and routines should be taught beginning on the first day of school and practiced during the first week until they become automatic. Classroom management needs to precede content instruction. Teachers need to have classroom management skills if student learning is going to occur. When establishing a learning environment, teachers will need to decide whether their classroom rules should be general or specific.

Specific Rules

Specific rules clearly address one action and state the expected student behavior. "Have all materials ready to use when the bell rings" is an example of a specific rule. Newer teachers may find specific rules helpful because they describe the expected student behavior. The disadvantage of specific rules is that more rules need to be created to handle all possible situations. It becomes more difficult to remember the rules when their number increases. Partin (2005) indicates that it is important not to try to cover every possible unacceptable behavior or students and teachers will become overwhelmed remembering all the rules. After the expected behavior is established, teachers can move from specific to more general rules (Wong & Wong, 2001).

General Rules

Experienced teachers may find general rules more useful. A general rule such as "Respect others" can be used in multiple situations and encompasses many specific rules. It could cover hitting, tattling, calling out, name calling, and a myriad of other situations. Wong and Wong (2001) recommend limiting the number of rules to about three to five so that your students can remember them. When students choose to abide by or break rules, there should be either positive or negative consequences. The most effective consequences are reasonable and logical. However, it is important that these consequences do not interfere with instruction. If students earn a penalty or reward, give it out immediately and quietly so that you can continue with the lesson, which is your goal.

Procedures and Routines

At times, coaches are called upon to help a teacher who has an understanding of how to establish classroom rules but little understanding of how to establish procedures and routines to help the class move along smoothly. Wong and Wong (2001) indicated that the "number one problem in the classroom is not discipline; it is the lack of procedures and routines" (p. 167). This difficulty can become particularly evident during transitions. A procedure is how the teacher wants something done. There is nothing inherently right or wrong about a procedure, and these procedures generally vary from teacher to teacher. Procedures include actions such as where to put your name on the paper, when to sharpen a pencil, and how to turn in your homework. To determine what procedures a teacher needs to establish, identify the recurring questions that students ask. These questions would be the areas for which the teacher needs to establish a procedure. Procedures increase on-task time and reduce classroom disruptions by telling the student how things are accomplished in the classroom.

In order to teach a procedure, begin by stating, explaining, modeling, and demonstrating it. Then have the students practice the procedure. Enough practice should be provided so that the procedure becomes a habit or a routine (Wong & Wong, 2001). Routines are what the students do automatically without prompting.

Individual Intervention Strategies

Sometimes individual students in your class might have more difficulty following the class rules than the rest of their class members do. This might be the time to consider an individual intervention strategy. This strategy will need to be tailored to meet the needs of the individual student, and it might take trial and error before you find an effective solution.

Point Sheets

A daily or weekly point sheet might be an effective method to provide behavioral support because it involves the student's caregivers in the behavior modification process. When implementing a point sheet, the student, the caregivers, and the teacher work together to determine a goal number of points to be earned by the student each day or week.

Desired behaviors or areas the student finds more difficult are identified. The example point sheet in appendix J includes the four classroom rules and a blank space to add a fifth rule that is individualized for the student. This fifth category would be an area where the student typically struggles to be successful. The point sheet is signed each day by the teacher indicating the number of points the student earned that day. The student takes the sheet home for the caregiver to sign. The points earned can be tied to agreed-upon rewards or consequences as

CHAPTER TWELVE

determined or agreed upon with all stakeholders (American Institutes for Research, 2015).

Observing a Student

A point sheet is an effective tool to use when you have identified the specific behavioral concerns. However, sometimes more information is required to determine the exact way to handle specific student concerns. You might need to determine the cause for specific behavior that seems to be keeping the student from making academic progress, or you might need to determine the frequency of specific behaviors. In each of these cases the goal is to increase the student's focus and attention to better meet the academic needs of the individual student.

ABC Chart

When attempting to determine the cause of specific behaviors, an ABC chart can be used (Hasbrouck & Denton, 2005). The Antecedent-Behavior-Consequence, or ABC, chart enables the teacher to determine the situations in which a student experiences difficulty. This observation tool is used to collect data about the event that precedes a specific behavior, its antecedent (A), the specific behavior of concern (B), and the consequence (C), or the event that immediately follows the behavior.

The use of an ABC chart can provide information about how to modify the classroom environment in an attempt to change the undesired behavior (University of Kansas, 2015). Including information about the time, subject area, and instructional setting, as is included in appendix K, might provide additional valuable information for analyzing the antecedent behavior. This information enables the teacher to determine the instructional format in which the behavior occurs: whole group, small group, or independent work. It will also provide information about the types of instructional activities, reading, writing, mathematics, and so forth that the student finds particularly frustrating.

Off-Task Behavior Chart

Now that the cause of the problem behavior has been examined, the teacher can implement specific interventions to address the area of concern. After intervention, it might be helpful to monitor progress by tracking the frequency of the behavior. This will provide information about whether the strategies that are being implemented are effectively changing and/or reducing the frequency of the off-task behavior.

The teacher might want to consider having the coach use an Off-Task Behavior Chart (appendix L). The individual student is observed for ten minutes. At thirty-second intervals the observer records whether the student is on task or off task. If the student is on task, a plus sign is recorded. If the student is off task, the specific type of off-task behavior is recorded. Off-task behavior is divided into three categories: inattentive, physically off task, and verbally off task. Inattentive activity would involve actions like daydreaming or looking around the room. Calling out, singing, humming, or talking to others would be coded as verbally off-task behavior. Physically off-task behavior would include actions such as playing with objects, getting out of the chair, walking around, or fighting.

Since the student's behavior is rated as off or on task twenty times, the percentage of off-task behavior can be calculated. Count up the total number of times the student was off task during the ten-minute period. If the child was off task fifteen times, you would calculate the percentage by dividing 15 by 20 and then multiplying by 100. In the previous example, the child would have been off task 75 percent of the time. This percentage could be compared over time to determine whether the amount of time on task is increasing. This would provide information about whether the intervention was effective.

The three types of off-task behaviors could also be compared by calculating the off-task percentage for each type of action. First count up the total number of *I*s that were recorded during the ten-minute observation. This will be the numerator of the fraction. Then count up the total number of times the student was off task; this will become the denominator of the fraction. Divide the numerator by the denominator and multiply by 100. The result is the percentage of time the student was inattentive. Follow the same procedure for each of the other categories. These percentages could be compared over time to determine whether the amount of time on task is increasing.

For example, if the student during the ten-minute observation was off task fifteen out of the twenty observations, we would then examine the results to determine how many times he was off task in each category. On his chart there were seven *I*s, five *V*s, and three *P*s recorded. To determine the I percentage, we would divide 7 by 15 and multiply by 100, which gives us 46 percent. The V percentage would be calculated by dividing 5 by 15 and multiplying by 100, which gives us 33 percent. The P percentage would be calculated by dividing 3 by 15 and multiplying by 100, which gives us 20 percent. We would then be able to compare these scores to the percentages he earned the next time he was observed. This type of an observation provides information about the frequency and type of off-task behavior.

Off-task behavior can be caused by many different factors. There might be a mismatch between the student's ability and the level of instruction. The work might be too difficult or too easy. The student might be concerned about factors outside of the school environment, such as events occurring in his home environment. Students could also be off task because the lesson is disorganized or poorly planned or presented because of a lack of procedures or rules. Making instruction orderly, predictable, and motivating makes it easier to hold students' attention most of the time.

Some general strategies that teachers can use to increase student attention would be to make the activities stimulating, provide choice, give clear directions, use proximity control, transition quickly, provide visual and kinesthetic support, and provide breaks to allow for students to refocus attention (Wright, 2015).

Reflect and Apply Activities

12.1. Talk to about five teachers in your school, and find out their classroom rules. Classify each rule as either specific or general. Discuss with the teachers why they decided on the rules they chose and how effectively they are working for them.

12.2. Observe a student either online or face-to-face using the ABC chart (appendix K). Determine what factors precipitate the behavior (A) and the consequence of the behavior (C).

12.3. Observe a student either online or face-to-face using the Off-Task Behavior Chart (appendix L). Determine the percentage and type of off-task behavior.

CHAPTER TWELVE

References

American Institutes for Research. (2015). *Point sheets/behavior report cards.* National Center on Intensive Intervention. Retrieved from http://www.intensiveintervention.org/sites/default/files/Point_Sheets.pdf.

Hasbrouck, J., & Denton, C. (2005). *The reading coach: A how-to-manual for success.* Longmont, CO: Sopris West.

Partin, R. L. (2005). *Classroom teacher's survival guide: Practical strategies, management techniques, and reproducibles for new and experienced teachers.* San Francisco, CA: Jossey-Bass.

University of Kansas. (2015). *Antecedent-behavior-consequence (ABC) chart.* Retrieved from http://www.specialconnections.ku.edu/?q=behavior_plans/functional_behavior_assessment/teacher_tools/antecedent_behavior_consequence_chart.

Wong, H. K., & Wong, R. T. (2001). *The first days of school: How to be an effective teacher.* Mountain View, CA: Harry K. Wong Publications.

Wright, J. (2015). *School-wide strategies for managing off-task/inattention.* Retrieved from http://www.jimwrightonline.com/php/interventionista/interventionista_intv_list.php?prob_type=off_task__inattention.

CHAPTER THIRTEEN

Jessie was in her office analyzing the results of the most recent round of progress monitoring. She had only been at this job half a year now, but she was starting to feel a lot more confident. The teachers were reaching out to her and becoming a little more receptive. The data from the December round of progress monitoring was the best they had seen so far. It was too early to tell, but those results seemed positive, Jessie thought hopefully, as her musings were interrupted by the phone ringing.

"Hello, Smith Elementary. Jessie Sedlack's office," Jessie said into the phone as she leaned across the piles of papers on her desk.

"Hi, my name is Lisa Conner. You don't know me, but the district office gave me your number. They said you would be the best person to talk to. I was just hired to start as the academic coach at New River Elementary School in January."

"Congratulations! That's exciting," Jessie responded.

"Well, I will agree it is exciting," Lisa commented, "but I am feeling a little overwhelmed as well. I am not exactly sure what I got myself into. Would you be willing to share with me what you know?"

"I am still new at this," Jessie replied, "but I can actually do one better. I will share with you what I wish I had known before I started this job. Then hopefully you won't make the same mistakes I made."

"That would be great. I really don't have any idea how to start this job," Lisa observed.

"Perhaps," suggested Jessie, "you would like to come over and shadow me for a couple of days, if it fits in your schedule."

CHAPTER THIRTEEN

"That would be wonderful. I was secretly hoping you would offer," Lisa confessed. "I would love to see what you are doing; it might give me a better handle on what I will need to do. When can we do that?"

"I already have some meetings set up for the end of this week. The teachers involved might feel uncomfortable having an observer sitting in their meeting. But I can do next week. I have a couple of days where I have classroom observations, PLC meetings, and some work with individual students. None of those are confidential, so that would be perfect."

"So, does next Tuesday work?"

"That would be great. Why don't you bring your computer so that you can save anything you find helpful?" Jessie suggested.

"I will. I'll see you Tuesday at 8:30. I am excited. This should be really helpful. Thanks so much," Lisa responded.

"No problem. See you then," Jessie said, hanging up the phone. *Who would have thought back in August that I would be feeling comfortable enough by December to help someone else make the transition to academic coach?*

Tips for Beginning Coaches

With one phone call, Jessie moved into a new phase of her coaching role. She is now in the role of coaching a new coach. Coaching a coach is similar to coaching a teacher, but there are some differences as well. To fill this role effectively, Jessie will need to be able to determine Lisa's needs and receptivity. Since Lisa made the phone call, she is obviously receptive to assistance and advice; this would be typical of new coaches. She will need advice about how to handle the challenges she has not faced in her previous position. Lisa has only a little bit of time before she starts her job, so she has a lot to learn in a very short period. Shadowing and conversations will be the first step. She will then probably add e-mails and phone calls. Jessie will probably spend a lot of time with Lisa at first, but as Lisa becomes more comfortable in her role, these interactions will become less frequent. In her new role as mentor, Jessie will also introduce Lisa to the other members of the district coaching team so that they can provide support as well.

Starting in a coaching position can be difficult. It is important to set up times for a new coach to shadow existing coaches at other schools and

CHAPTER THIRTEEN

to meet with them to discuss procedures and concerns. It would be helpful to set up a regular scheduled time to allow the new coach to gradually locate information, plan, and get answers to pressing questions.

Even though you have talked with other coaches, remember that the role of the coach may differ from school to school. The first step should be a conversation between the principal and the coach to review what has been happening at the school and what next steps should be. This will help to flesh out the role of the coach in this particular school.

You might need to win over the faculty so that they see you as a resource and not as an evaluator. Consequently, sometimes as a coach, because of teacher resistance, you will need to drum up business. There is bound to be some resistance to a new person in any position. Change can be hard. Teachers are concerned about what it means to have a coach and whether you are there to help them or evaluate them. They also might not be exactly sure what your new role entails.

A great first step for any new coach is to advertise. You may need to market your services. Teachers might not know what you are supposed to do or can do. To help the transition to go more smoothly, you may want to create printed flyers or pamphlets that explain your role, schedule, availability, and what you can do to help the teachers.

Remember that a new position can be hard. Start small. You will want to begin by working with the colleagues who are willing to work with you. Go to your colleagues. Stop by their classrooms. It is much easier to go to them than to get them to come to you. In your first "getting to know you" visits, begin by chatting and building relationships. The easiest way to do this is to ask general questions. Ask about their students and their accomplishments. Encourage each staff member to share their successes. Try to initiate some kind of contact with each teacher at least once a month, regardless of the teacher's interest or readiness. Determine whether there is anything that the teacher is doing that you should learn about and perhaps share with other teachers (Spaulding & Smith, 2012).

As you are making these contacts, continue advertising. Remember to give credit to others and to recognize their contributions toward increasing student achievement. Stress collaboration rather than the fact that you are an expert. Remember to emphasize the shared process and what others are accomplishing. This will help to reduce the "expert aura." Schedule a monthly check-in with each teacher. This is your opportunity to develop a relationship. During this session, ask three questions: "What is working well for you? Do you have a concern about any of your students' progress? Do you have any questions or suggestions for me so that I can serve you more effectively?" (Hasbrouck & Denton, 2005, p. 27).

Don't separate your role from that of a teacher. Keep your role as similar to the teacher's as you can. The best way to do this might be to stress in every conversation that it is all about the students and their achievement. The coach and the teachers are working together to reach the same goal—improved student achievement.

Generally, teachers are more willing to work with you if they see you as one of them. An easy way to accomplish this might be to volunteer to work with small groups of students in the teacher's classroom. This would be an effective way to demonstrate a skill or strategy.

Be available to listen. Schedule time to go into classrooms (Spaulding & Smith, 2012). When you are done, leave thank-you notes after you visit a teacher's room. Thank teachers for inviting you into their room, for sharing their students, and for sharing their instructional practice. Let the teachers know how much you appreciate all they are doing for students.

Because you need to be ready to help all teachers, it will be important to study the curriculum and the assessment materials. You will need to know the standards for each content and grade level you coach.

Developing Skills

Throughout this book we have discussed many skills that coaches require. Coaches require the ability to:

- Determine the appropriate level of coaching needed.
- Reinforce research-based best practices.
- Collect, organize, and analyze data.
- Promote teacher and student growth.
- Encourage collaboration between teachers.
- Identify additional resources to help others be successful.
- Support and enhance school goals.

CHAPTER THIRTEEN

Coaching Support

As the coach you are responsible for helping teachers to refine and extend their ability to use instructional practices effectively. This can be accomplished through coaching, matching teachers together so that they can be involved in peer coaching, forming small groups of teachers who are interested in studying a specific topic, involving teachers in action research, or providing workshops to address specific skills or concepts. Teachers need to decide on the instructional practices they will use. There are many different methods to choose from: direct teaching, demonstration, Socratic method, cooperative learning, simulations and games, and drill and practice, just to name a few.

Sousa (2011) identifies nine components of a lesson plan that should be considered: the anticipatory set, learning objectives, purpose, input, modeling, check for understanding, guided practice, closure, and independent practice.

Professional Development to Change Practice

Professional development has traditionally been the way to improve teacher effectiveness. It was assumed that providing the training would result in a changed attitude, which would then result in a change in the teacher's practice. However, Guskey's work (2002) determined that aiming professional development at changing teachers' attitudes about a practice will not result in lasting change—especially in the current environment of increased accountability. Instead, it is important to show teachers the impact of the strategy on their students. Teachers are rightfully concerned about switching out an effective strategy for a new one they learn about that might not be as effective. Therefore, in order to create change in teaching practices, teachers need to see the benefits of the change for their students. This is why field-testing the evidence-based strategies in their own classrooms is important. Training sessions should be brief and focused on one specific skill or strategy that can be used in multiple settings.

Spaulding and Smith (2012) developed a process for bringing about building-wide change:

1. Identify the strategies currently used and additional strategies you think might be effective.

2. Determine who will deliver the training on one of these strategies and how it will be delivered.

3. Create specific, focused professional development training on one strategy. Make sure that the principal attends so that administrative support is demonstrated.

4. The coach and the teachers should work together to implement the strategy in the classrooms.

5. Teachers share with each other the data they have collected about the effectiveness of the strategy.

6. Finally, determine whether more training is needed and whether the strategy was effective.

Coaches make a difference in the lives of teachers and students. Go ahead make a difference. Be a change agent!

Reflect and Apply Activities

13.1. Create a flyer to introduce yourself to the faculty of the school where you will be working as a coach. Make sure to include what you can do for the faculty, your availability, and how they can contact you.

13.2. There are many different types of teacher contacts. Develop a form for tracking the frequency and type of contacts for your school. Make sure to include each staff member's name, dates, and a key for recording the type of contact.

13.3. Create a pamphlet that you could share with a newly appointed coach helping them to make the transition into coaching. Include important information they should know and additional resources they would want to be aware of.

References

Guskey, T. R. (2002). Professional development and teacher change. *Teachers and Teaching: Theory and Practice, 8*(3), 381–91.

CHAPTER THIRTEEN

Hasbrouck, J., & Denton, C. (2005). *The reading coach: A how-to manual for success*. Longmont, CO: Sopris West.

Sousa, D. A. (2011). *How the brain learns* (4th ed.). Thousand Oaks, CA: Corwin.

Spaulding, D. T., & Smith, G. (2012). *Instructional coaches and the instructional leadership team: A guide for school-building improvement*. Thousand Oaks, CA: Corwin.

APPENDIX A
Evaluating Instruction Short-Term Memory Checklist

Presentation Factors

1. _____ Information presented is limited to three to five chunks.

2. _____ Participants shift the way they are working with the information after ten to twenty minutes.

3. _____ Approximately ten- to twenty-minute limit on working with the same information at the same level.

4. _____ Humor is used to increase physiological and psychological benefits.

5. _____ Movement and kinesthetic learning is incorporated.

6. _____ Opportunities for group and individual reflection are provided.

7. _____ Teacher monitors attention and engagement through proximity.

Environmental Factors

1. _____ Variety of grouping methods are used.

2. _____ Distractions are kept to a minimum.

APPENDIX A

Learner Factors

1. _____ Learner self-concept is supported during learning.

2. _____ Learner accountability for the information is embedded in the presentation.

3. _____ Formative assessments are used to provide learner feedback.

4. _____ Learner's level of concern is not too high or too low.

5. _____ Learner misunderstandings are clarified.

APPENDIX B
Evaluating Instruction Short- and Long-Term Memory Checklist

Presentation Factors

1. _____ Information presented is limited to three to five chunks.

2. _____ Participants shift the way they are working with the information after ten to twenty minutes.

3. _____ Approximately ten- to twenty-minute limit on working with the same information at the same level.

4. _____ Humor is used to increase physiological and psychological benefits.

5. _____ Movement and kinesthetic learning is incorporated.

6. _____ Opportunities for group and individual reflection are provided.

7. _____ Teacher monitors attention and engagement through proximity.

Environmental Factors

1. _____ Variety of grouping methods are used.

2. _____ Distractions are kept to a minimum.

APPENDIX B

Learner Factors

1. _____ Learner self-concept is supported during learning.

2. _____ Learner accountability for the information is embedded in the presentation.

3. _____ Formative assessments are used to provide learner feedback.

4. _____ Learner's level of concern is not too high or too low.

5. _____ Learner misunderstandings are clarified.

Long-Term Memory Checklist

1. _____ Rote rehearsal is included.

2. _____ Elaborative rehearsal is included.

3. _____ Serial position effect is considered in placement of important information.

4. _____ Varied instruction strategies are used.

5. _____ Cueing system is provided for ease of retrieval.

6. _____ Gradual release of information is used.

7. _____ Opportunities for reflection are provided.

8. _____ Instruction is presented in a logical order to create general and specific schemata.

APPENDIX C
Checklist for Moran's Continuum of Learning Formats

Activity	Tally Frequency per Week	% of Frequency for Each Activity
Collaborative Resource Manager		
Workshop/PD Presenter		
Classroom Visits		
Co-planner		
Study Group Facilitator		
Present Demonstration Lessons		
Peer Coach		
Co-teacher		
Total		

APPENDIX C

1. Record activity for a single week.
2. In the middle column place a tally mark each time an activity occurs during that week.
3. Add the number of tally marks together and record the total in the space at the bottom of the column.
4. Calculate the percentage of frequency by dividing the number of tally marks in each category by the total number of activities described each week, and then multiply by 100 to determine the percentage of frequency for each activity.

APPENDIX D
Basic Literacy Data-Collection Tool

Directions: In each row, record the name of a student in your class. In the State Assessment column record the student's scores from the previous year's state assessment. Progress monitoring is often completed three times a year, which is why there are three columns under Progress Monitoring. The score from each progress-monitoring assessment is recorded in the appropriate column.

The scores from an Informal Reading Inventory (IRI) can provide additional information to inform instruction. Multiple columns are provided so that academic growth between assessments can be compared. If the scores from the three assessments (the state assessment, progress monitoring, and IRI) indicate concerns, the next four columns provide places to record scores from formal or informal diagnostic basic skill assessments. Four of the basic skills of the reading process are listed. Comprehension is not included because the state assessment, the progress-monitoring assessments, and the IRI all provide information about the student's comprehension levels.

	Progress Monitoring			Informal Reading Inventory			Operations and Algebraic Thinking			Phonemic Awareness			Phonics			Fluency			Vocabulary		
	1	2	3	1	2	3	1	2	3	1	2	3	1	2	3	1	2	3	1	2	3
State Assessment																						
Student																						

APPENDIX E
Literacy Data Collection by Standard

Directions: In each row, record the name of a student in your class. In the State Assessment column record the student's scores from the previous year's state assessment. Progress monitoring is often completed three times a year, which is why there are three columns under Progress Monitoring. The score from each progress-monitoring assessment is recorded in the appropriate column.

The scores from an Informal Reading Inventory (IRI) can provide additional information to inform instruction. Multiple columns are provided so that academic growth between assessments can be compared. If the scores from the three assessments (the state assessment, progress monitoring, and IRI) indicate concerns, the next five columns provide places to record scores from formal or informal standards assessments based upon the Common Core State Standard.

Language	Vocabulary Acquisition									
Language	Knowledge of Conventions									
Speaking and Listening	Presentation									
Speaking and Listening	Comprehension and Collaboration									
Writing	Range of Writing									
Writing	Research									
Writing	Production and Distribution									
Informational and Literary Texts	Text Types and Purposes									
Informational and Literary Texts	Range and Complexity									
Informational and Literary Texts	Integration									
Informational and Literary Texts	Craft and Structure									
Foundational Skills K–5	Key Ideas and Details									
Foundational Skills K–5	Fluency									
Foundational Skills K–5	Phonics and Word Recognition									
Foundational Skills K–5	Phonological Awareness									
Foundational Skills K–5	Print Concepts									
IRI	3									
IRI	2									
IRI	1									
Progress Monitoring	3									
Progress Monitoring	2									
Progress Monitoring	1									
State Assessment										
Name										

APPENDIX F
K–5 Mathematics Data-Collection Tool

Directions: In each row, record the name of a student in your class. In the State Assessment column record the student's scores from the previous year's state assessment. Progress monitoring is often completed three times a year, which is why there are three columns under Progress Monitoring. The score from each progress-monitoring assessment is recorded in the appropriate column.

The next six columns provide places to record scores from three assessments across the six domains of the Common Core Mathematics Standards so that you can monitor progress across the standards to guide instruction.

	Progress Monitoring			Counting and Cardinality			Operations and Algebraic Thinking			Numbers and Operations in Base 10			Numbers and Operations: Fractions			Measurement and Data			Geometry		
	1	2	3	1	2	3	1	2	3	1	2	3	1	2	3	1	2	3	1	2	3
State Assessment																					
Student																					

APPENDIX G
6–8 Mathematics Data-Collection Tool

Directions: In each row, record the name of a student in your class. In the State Assessment column, record the student's scores from the previous year's state assessment. Progress monitoring is often completed three times a year, which is why there are three columns under Progress Monitoring. The score from each progress-monitoring assessment is recorded in the appropriate column.

The next six columns provide places to record scores from three assessments across the six domains of the Common Core Mathematics Standards so that you can monitor progress across the standards to guide instruction.

	Progress Monitoring			Ratios and Proportional Relationships			The Number System			Expressions and Equations			Functions			Geometry			Statistics and Probability		
	1	2	3	1	2	3	1	2	3	1	2	3	1	2	3	1	2	3	1	2	3
State Assessment																						
Student																						

APPENDIX H
Environmental Observation Form

Physical Environment

Lighting is comfortable and adequate.	
Noise level is appropriate.	
Temperature level is appropriate.	
Classroom routines occur smoothly.	
Arrangement encourages student interactions.	
There is ease of traffic flow around the room.	
Tripping hazards are not evident.	
Walls relate to instructional content.	
Student work is displayed.	

Social/Cultural Environment

Teacher–student interactions are calm and supportive.	
Peer interactions are calm and supportive.	
Attitude of respect and rapport is evident.	
Expected behavior is clearly described.	

APPENDIX H

Classroom climate is open and accepting.	
Materials reflect students' cultural backgrounds.	
Classroom disruptions are handled calmly.	
High expectations are set for all learners.	
Student comfort level is evident.	

Instructional Environment

Materials are organized and readily available.	
Students are actively involvement with instructional content.	
Differentiation and/or modifications are provided.	
Various instructional groupings are used.	
Different modalities of presentation are addressed.	
Transitions occur smoothly.	
Learning and growth is valued.	
Students show pride in their work.	

APPENDIX I
Higher-Order Question Stems and Projects

Analyzing

What event would probably not have happened?
If _____ happened, how might the ending have changed?
How is _____ similar to _____?
What was the turning point of the story?
What motive did _____ have for _____?
What is the relationship between _____ and _____?
What inferences can you make about _____?
Have we left out any important information?
What is the most important idea?
What are the strongest points the speaker/author makes?

Analyzing Projects

Use a Venn diagram to show how two topics are similar and different.
Design a questionnaire to gather information about _____.
Make a flow chart to show the stages of_____.
Construct a graph to illustrate _____.
Review a work of art.
Role-play a conversation with the character or historic figure.
Construct a decision-making matrix.

APPENDIX I

Evaluating

Is there a better solution to _____?
How would you have handled _____?
What changes to _____ would you recommend?
How effective are _____?
What are the pros and cons of _____?
Who will profit from this decision?
How could you verify _____?
What are the alternatives to the solution chosen?
What would you have done?
Can we trust the source of this material?

Evaluating Projects

Construct a list of criteria to judge the appropriateness of the solution.
Evaluate a character's actions.
Debate both sides of the issue.
Prepare and present a persuasive presentation to change the situation.
Research other possible solutions to this problem.
Identify additional issues related to the problem that the author did not explore.

Creating

Can you design a _____ to _____?
Can you propose a possible solution to _____?
What would happen if _____?
How many ways can you _____?
Can you create a new and unusual use for _____?
How would you generate a plan to _____?

Creating Projects

Invent a machine to _____.
Use an analogy or metaphor to describe or compare this to something else.

APPENDIX I

Create a new solution to this problem.
Write a show or multimedia creation about _____.
Sell the idea to a new audience.
Design a book, magazine, or advertisement about this topic.
Devise a way to _____.

APPENDIX J
Weekly Point Sheet

Name _____
Week of _____

Subject	Goal 1	Goal 2	Goal 3	Goal 4	Goal 5

APPENDIX J

Daily Total

Goal 1: Is polite and helpful.	Monday _____
Goal 2: Respects others.	Tuesday _____
Goal 3: Completes work on time.	Wednesday _____
Goal 4: Follows directions the first time they are given.	Thursday _____
Goal 5: _____	Friday _____

Parent Signature _____

APPENDIX K
ABC Chart

Student _____ Date _____ Observer _____
Behaviors of Concern: _____

Time	Instructional Activity Subject and Format	Antecedent	Behavior	Consequence

APPENDIX K

This chart can be used to address classroom behaviors the teacher has identified as problematic.

In the first two columns, record the time and the setting in which the behavior occurs.

In the fourth column, describe the actual behavior as it is exhibited.

In the fifth column, record the teacher's or other students' response to the behavior.

The third column may be a little more difficult to complete. Try to describe exactly what happened before the problematic behavior occurred.

After the chart is completed, analyze the data to determine triggers for the behavior and the typical responses to the behavior.

Sharing this information may help the teacher to determine ways to intervene before the problematic behavior occurs.

APPENDIX L
Off-Task Behavior Chart

Observe the student for ten minutes. At each thirty-second interval, quickly record the type of off-task behavior or make a + sign if the student is on task. Use the following abbreviations to describe the off-task behavior: I – Inattentive; P – Physically off task; V – Verbally off task.

Time	Type of Off-Task Behavior	Description of Behavior
0:30		
1:00		
1:30		
2:00		
2:30		
3:00		
3:30		
4:00		
4:30		
5:00		
5:30		
6:00		
6:30		
7:00		
7:30		
8:00		

APPENDIX L

Time	Type of Off-Task Behavior	Description of Behavior
8:30		
9:00		
9:30		
10:00		

Calculate the Percentage in Each Category

Percent of **total** off-task behavior = total # of times off task / 20 × 100 _____

Percent of **Inattentive** off-task behavior = # of **I** / total # of off-task behaviors × 100 _____

Percent of **Verbal** off-task behaviors = # of **V** / total # of off-task behaviors × 100 _____

Percent of **Physical** off-task behaviors = # of **P** / total # of off-task behaviors × 100 _____

INDEX

ABC chart, 145, 179–80
accountability, 31, 34, 86, 153
action research, 43, 136–38
administration, 3, 4, 9, 22, 40, 72, 84, 87, 136, 137–38
adult learning theory, 24, 43, 82–83; andragogy, 82; content-based focus on, 95–96; self-directed, 82–83; transformative, 83
anxiety, helpful, 31
assessments, 23, 65–69, 163–70; criterion-referenced, 66, 73; diagnostic, 67–68, 69, 100; evaluative, 68; formal, 65–68; informal, 23, 65, 67, 68–69, 73, 84, 87, 99, 109; norm-referenced, 66, 73; outcome, 68, 86, 108; progress monitoring, 7, 43, 68, 69, 70, 163, 165, 167, 169; reliable, 66–67; screening, 23, 66, 67; standardized, 66, 86; summative, 40, 65, 67, 68, 85; valid, 66–67, 68

behavior strategies, 142–47, 157–60, 179–80, 181–82; proximity control, 33–34; transitions, 84, 125, 143; visual and kinesthetic support, 125, 147
Bloom's taxonomy, 133–35

classroom environment, instructional, 89, 124–25, 127, 145, 172; differentiation, 24, 29, 124–25; modalities, 52, 125; organization, 124; student achievement, 4, 10, 17, 65, 85, 94, 96, 125, 126, 137, 138, 142, 151, 152; student involvement, 124; transitions, 125, 143
classroom environment, physical, 89, 119–21, 127, 145, 171; lighting, 119–20; noise, 120; room arrangement, 120–21; temperature, 120; traffic flow, 121; visual displays, 121
classroom environment, social/cultural, 89, 121–24, 127, 171–72; classroom management, 123–24, 142; multicultural materials, 123; peer interactions, 122; respect,

INDEX

122–23; student expectations, 123; teacher–student interactions, 122

classroom management, 18, 19, 89, 106, 123, 142–47, 171–72; procedures, 125, 142, 143–44, 147; routines, 24, 85, 121, 122, 124, 125, 142, 143, 144; rules, 123, 142–43, 144, 147

coach, effective, 18–24, 38–39, 109–10; and adult learning, 19, 24, 96, 97; assessment skills, 23; beliefs, 18–19, 39; coaching skills, 18–20, 39; content expertise, 18, 19, 22, 39, 96, 97, 152; curricular standards, 97, 152; data analysis, 39–40, 42, 96; differentiation skills, 23–24, 39; grade level, 40, 65, 84, 98, 120, 125, 152; leadership skills, 18, 19, 22, 39; literacy skills, 22–23, 126; relationship skills, 18, 19, 22, 39, 151; school reform, 21, 22, 39; teacher relationships, 39, 109, 110, 151; teaching expertise, 18, 19; writing skills, 23, 39

coaches, characteristics of, 18–20, 21, 38–39

coaches, preparing beginning, 150–52; mentor, 3–4, 150; shadowing, 150

coaching, general information, 2–5; components of, 21–24; continuum, 59–61; definitions of, 3–4; effectiveness of, 46; schedule, 151, 152

coaching, methods for, 59–61, 98, 136; cooperative learning, 153; co-planning, 58, 59; co-teaching, 55, 59, 61, 85; demonstration lesson, 59, 153; drill, 40, 153; expert, 3, 4, 5, 60, 98, 126, 138, 151; facilitator, 5, 60, 83; monthly check-in, 151–52; observational categories, 84–85; resource manager, 60; simulations and games, 153; Socratic method, 153; study groups, 58, 59, 60; visits, 59, 60, 98, 151, 152

coaching, types of, 2, 57–59; clinical supervision, 59; cognitive, 22, 44, 58, 105; collaborative problem solver, 5, 136; formal literacy, 2, 58; informal, 2, 57–58; mixed model, 58; peer coaching and mentoring, 58, 98, 136

coaching systems, components of, 94–97; conditions that support, 96; content-based focus, 95–96; instructional leadership, 97

cognitive process, 51, 78

convergent thinking, 133

data collection/analysis, 39–40, 42, 65–73, 85; class, 40, 41, 69; district, 69; school, 38, 69, 96; student, 60, 65, 69–70, 71; teacher, 71–73

data disaggregation, 40–42; classroom level, 40, 65; cohort analysis, 41, 65; longitudinal analysis, 42, 65; trend analysis, 40–41, 65

digital natives, 104–7; complex texts, 105–6; humor, 106; movement, 106–7; novelty, 106; task switching, 105

distractions, 30, 31, 104

divergent thinking, 133

emotions, role of, 51, 134

endorphins, 33, 106

feedback, 31, 99–101, 125–27; corrective, 100; grade level, 37,

40, 65, 84, 126; instructional scaffolding, 99–100; specific praise, 99; structuring, 126–27; wait time, 100, 112, 134
formative assessments, 31
functional magnetic resonance imaging (fMRI), 70–71

Gardner's intelligences, 80–81; bodily-kinesthetic intelligence, 81; existential intelligence, 81; interpersonal intelligence, 81; intrapersonal intelligence, 81; logical-mathematical intelligence, 80; musical intelligence, 81; naturalistic intelligence, 81; spatial-visual intelligence, 81; verbal-linguistic intelligence, 80
growth mindset, 5–9, 12; developing, 6–7, 10; hindrances to, 7–8

higher-order thinking, 133–34, 173–75
humor, 33, 106

individual intervention strategies, 144–47; ABC chart, 145; observation, 145; off-task behavior chart, 145–47; point sheets, 144–45
information retrieval, 30, 32, 44, 50, 53–54, 79, 80, 107
instructional leadership, 9, 12, 97
inter-rater reliability, 137

Kosc, 2

learning styles, 78–80, 81; auditory, 80; kinesthetic, 79, 80; visual, 79, 80

listening skills, 110–11; focused, 111; global, 111; internal, 110; verbal, 112
long-term memory, 31, 32–33, 44–46, 50, 61, 107, 160; episodic, 44, 45; declarative, 44, 45; implicit, 45, 51; nondeclarative, 44, 45–46; procedural, 44, 45; semantic, 44, 45

memory. *See* long-term memory; short-term memory; working memory
mentor, 3–4, 150
minimal encouragers, 112, 114
mnemonic devices, 32
modeling, 28, 32, 33, 42, 55, 58, 114, 122, 123, 125, 144
movement, 33, 79, 81, 106–7, 120, 121
multitasking, 105

National Board of Professional Teaching Standards, 85–86
neuro synapses, 43–44

observation: categories, 84–85; of classrooms, 85, 87; data from, 85–86; feedback after, 125–27; and individual intervention, 145; protocols, 84
off-task behavior chart, 145–47, 181–82

point sheets, 144–45, 177–78
positive learning climate, 33, 50, 51, 106
practice, 53, 54, 56, 87, 89, 96, 100, 105, 114, 125, 134, 144, 153
professional development, 3, 5, 7, 28, 31, 37, 42–43, 51, 52, 73, 78, 81,

INDEX

83–84, 87, 96, 97; collaboration, 60, 121, 137, 151, 152; data analysis, 55, 57, 60; gradual release, 54–57, 85, 100; reflection, 57
professional learning communities (PLCs), 42, 109, 136

questioning, 16, 51, 95, 99, 113–14, 132

retention: elaborative rehearsal, 51–52; multisensory, 52–53, 106, 107; rote rehearsal, 51, 52; time, 107, 110
retention, strategies for, 51–53, 107–9; games, 52, 106–7, 153; jigsaw, 52; journal, 52, 70; music, 45, 81, 106, 107; role-playing, 52, 56

scaffolding, 99–100
schemata, 50, 51, 108; general, 32, 44; specific, 32, 44
self-concept, 33
senses, 29, 30, 53
short-term memory, 29–31, 32, 44, 46, 50, 61, 157–58, 159–60; environmental factors, 157, 159; immediate memory, 30; learner, 31, 158, 160; presentation, 31, 52, 125, 157, 159. *See also* working memory
silence, 112, 113

SMART goals, 10–11
SOLER, 111
student-focused coaching model, 4
study groups, roles within, 58, 59, 60
supervision, 20–21, 59
survey, 71–73; anonymous/identified, 72; structuring questions, 72–73; question order, 73; response type, 72

teacher categories, 28–29, 97–98, 135–37; eager and open, 28, 97, 98; eager but resistant, 28, 97; reluctant and resistant, 28–29, 98; reluctant but not resistant, 28, 97–98
teacher effectiveness, 16–18; by teacher perception, 16–17; by student achievement, 17–18
teacher evaluation systems, 86–88, 95–96, 118–19; Danielson, 87, 95, 99, 108, 119; Marshall, 87, 95, 108, 119; Marzano, 87–88, 96, 108, 119; McRel, 88, 95, 108, 119
teacher resistance, 135–37, 138, 151
top-down process, 135–36
transfer, 29, 79, 107

working memory, 30–31, 33, 54, 105; central control mechanism, 30; phonological loop, 30; visuospatial sketchpad, 30; level of concern, 31

ABOUT THE AUTHORS

Lin Carver, PhD, is a professor, literacy coach, author, and presenter with more than forty years of experience at the K–12 and university levels in both face-to-face and online formats. Dr. Carver is the reading program administrator at Saint Leo University, where she has been for the past seven years. She is active in supporting the local K–12 school district and literacy associations; conducting research in the areas of literacy, technology, and student engagement; and presenting both nationally and internationally.

Judith Orth, PhD, is a pedagogical professional with more than forty-five years of experience in public and higher education. She has a plentitude of publications and educational experience in the elementary/middle school classroom and as a public school administrator, university professor, and university administrator, in both physical and online academic institutions. Dr. Orth has presented at conferences, workshops, and seminars, and she has been affiliated with Walden University for more than twelve years. She is very active in local literacy foundations as well as national reading/educational associations.

www.ingramcontent.com/pod-product-compliance
Lightning Source LLC
Chambersburg PA
CBHW030138240426
43672CB00005B/178